Crushing Soft Rubies

A Memoir

• 10th ANNIVERSARY EDITION •

Janet Stickmon

BROKEN SHACKLE PUBLISHING • Oakland

ACKNOWLEDGMENTS

This book would not have been possible without the love and support of my parents, Lucrecia Mendoza and Fermon Stickmon, Jr., Dominga and Cipriano Navaja, Alison, Martin, JoAnna, and Chris Rodriguez, Emerita and Scott Caballero, Lula Bible, Charles Stickmon, Diana, Tom, Katie, Anna, and Louis Shepardson, Mely Tabasa, Dolores Weidemann, Lisa Directo, Gigi and David Chow, Dion Manly, Glenn Noronha, and Gerardo Aldana. Thanks to David Huang for his photography, to James Cagney Jr. for editing first edition, to Uncle Fred Cordova and Mama Vangie Canonizado Buell for their support and guidance, to Luisa Penaranda, Oscar Penaranda and Edelyn Mendoza for helping me with the glossary, to Estria Miyashiro and Poonam Whabi of Tumi's Design for original book design, and to Poonam Whabi of Design Action Collective for book cover updates. Thank you to Barbara Hazzard, the Hesed Community, and all donors for their financial support. To my husband, Shawn Taylor, who was loving and supportive throughout the four years I spent writing this book and to our daughter who was born a few years after its release. Lastly, I am indebted to God and all the ancestors who guide me daily.

1

There were no streetlights on East Avenue G. Only the moon and the headlights of Momma's Ford Fairmont lit the pavement ahead. The arid land of the Mojave Desert stretched for miles with tumbleweeds scattered on both sides of the single-lane road. Only nine houses were on this street, and after passing the first house, my mother and I saw fire trucks parked at one of the houses up ahead.

"It looks like they're in front of the Jacksons' house," I said.

Momma drove a little closer and said, "Or maybe they're at Mr. John's or Ms. Mae's house." We passed each house one by one, holding our breath. The possibilities were narrowing down. None of our neighbors' homes were on fire. The fire trucks were parked in front of our house.

Momma pulled over. I jumped out of the car and ran toward our house. Momma was somewhere behind me. Smoke rose from the rooftop, and the stench of burning cinders filled the air. Our dogs were running loose, barking. Neighbors and strangers gathered around, watching the fire. Flashes of red and white light from the fire trucks reflected off their faces. In a panic, I fought my way through the crowd asking anyone if they knew where my Daddy was. No one answered.

A few feet ahead, I saw him standing alone. "Daddy!!" I yelled as I rushed toward him. He saw us and opened his arms. Momma and I hugged him so tight, crying as we held him.

"What happened?" we asked.

"I was out in the yard," he stammered, "watering the garden, when something exploded from the middle of the house. Then the house was on fire. I let the dogs loose, and Ms. Lynn called the fire station." Daddy held his face in his hands. Momma was silent. All of us stood and looked at our house. From the front, its white walls were still white. Its pine green trim, still green. We saw no flames. But we knew the fire was eating away at the inside by the black smoke it was spitting out.

About a half hour passed. A fireman told my parents the fire was out, but the house was almost completely destroyed. "It won't be safe to go in," he said, "since there's a risk the fire could start up again. Tomorrow you can salvage what you can." With those words, he handed my father a small brown envelope. "If you bring this to the bank, you can exchange it for undamaged bills." In the envelope was a small stack of money with the edges burnt off. He must have found it under my father's mattress, where he usually kept his money.

The three of us spent the night at Ms. Lynn's house next door. My parents and Ms. Lynn were busy talking and making phone calls. I sat on the couch scared to find out what the fire consumed and what it spared.

That night, June 12, 1986, I learned what it meant for things to be impermanent. Yes, I was very happy my parents weren't in that house, but I couldn't help but think about all the material things I lost. The thought of doing without the things my little 12 year-old self was used to having made me panic, "What if all my clothes are gone? What if my flute melted? I won't be able to join the band next year! What if I lost all my friends' phone numbers? I won't have anyone to talk to all summer!" And another voice kept telling me, "Things in this world just don't last forever," and I hated those words. I prayed that night that God would at least leave behind something I could keep.

As for my parents, I knew that this was much more than a lesson in impermanence. I didn't understand everything they were going through at the time, but I did know they didn't expect this from life. My mother dreamt of coming to the United States and living a better life away from her family in the Philippines. My father hopped freight trains from Louisiana to California to do construction work and at the very least, dreamt of having more money. Even though they didn't make much money outside my father's Social Security checks, I could sense Momma and Daddy believed things would get better.

Up until this moment, life seemed good for us. My parents found enough work to keep food on the table, pay the bills, and pay for all my activities at school. I was having a great time in junior high, meeting new friends in the band and on the track team. We were poor, but we had our modest belongings, our friends, and each other. There was no indication that this was just the beginning of a series of changes that would test our desire to live. There was only my parents' anticipation for a better life. And my mother, especially, looked forward to a better life for her only child.

2

One of Inday Lucy's coworkers, Maria, offered to put her address in a magazine so she could find an American penpal. Fermon found the address and began writing to her. However, he didn't know that the woman who was responding to his first couple of letters was not Inday Lucy, but was Maria. It wasn't until after a few letters were exchanged that Inday Lucy actually wrote to Fermon.

In his letters, Fermon told her that he had written to many women before and never told them he was Black. When he eventually did, they stopped writing. Lucy couldn't understand how people could be so filled with hate towards someone who was Black. Touched by Fermon's words, she decided not to be like those other women.

Only Inday Lucy and Fermon knew how long they exchanged love letters and postcards. Besides Lucy's coworker, no one in Labangon knew my mom had a penpal in the United States until he flew to the Philippines to visit her.

In 1970, Fermon came to her home while she was downtown with Auntie Adela, her sister-in-law and close friend. As they walked home, a neighbor came running down the street saying, "Oh! Inday Lucy. There's a foreigner at your house. He came to see you!" She became very nervous and walked faster with each step. Meanwhile, her father and Fermon were sitting outside talking and enjoying each other's company. Inday's father, my *lolo*, was quite impressed with Fermon since he flew all the way from the United States just to meet his youngest daughter.

One of Inday's sisters, Lita, was yelling insults at my father from across the street, "A buffalo! An American buffalo!"

My father looked up and asked, "What did she say?"

Lolo didn't answer. Somehow, they just returned to where they left off in their conversation.

Inday Lucy now walked cautiously down the dirt road toward home. Lucy, being slightly embarrassed, tried avoiding her father and Fermon by running past the house to go hide. Fermon saw her and yelled, "Oh, Lucy!" She stopped, turned around, and approached the both of them, not knowing what to expect since she had told no one in the family that she had been writing to a man overseas.

⁜

On June 15, 1970, Lucrecia Navaja Mendoza married Fermon Stickmon, Jr. She was 33 and he was 58. They left the Philippines and came to the United States to start their life together in Yuba City, California. Mom left her job at the City Hall in Cebu, left her family, left the *barangay* of Labangon. She left all that was familiar to her so she could live a new life in a foreign culture married to an African-American man whose culture she would soon learn. Dad was in a familiar environment, starting a new relationship with a Filipino woman whose culture and traditions he, too, had yet to learn. The couple looked forward to working hard and sharing a lifetime together, in spite of the 25 years that separated them.

Their first child was born Friday, August 25, 1972—just a year and a month before I was born. When I stumbled upon her birth certificate as a child, a barrage of questions left my mouth, "You had a daughter before me?

What was her name? Where is she? What happened to her?"

My mother patiently answered my first few questions, knowing that most of the information could have been found on the birth certificate. "Her name was Sharon. She lived for about 3 days and died of respiratory problems. I didn't have natural childbirth. But with you, I did." That was it. As I continued to ask questions she abruptly said, "I don't want to talk about it." So, I stopped and sought out clues for myself.

Sharon Catherine Stickmon was born at 11:55 a.m. and weighed 7 lbs., 13 oz. and was 20 in. long. I studied her footprints and handprints on her birth certificate, gently tracing my fingers along the curves her imprint made, missing the older sister I never met, trying to imagine how life would be with Sharon.

On September 25, 1973, at 10:26 p.m., Mom gave birth to another baby girl. Born at Fremont Medical Center in Yuba City, I weighed 5 lbs. 12.5 oz. and was 19.5 in. long. Even though Daddy wanted to name me Sally Mae, Momma preferred Janet, and so I was named Janet Christine Stickmon. My original birth certificate indicated that both of my parents were Caucasian, something they were both very angry about. In 1984, they filed a correction to my birth certificate to show that my father was African-American and my mother was Filipino.

Coming into the world, I had no idea how much my birth meant to my parents, particularly my mother. In time, I would become the one to inherit their unfulfilled dreams that would not only be fulfilled through me but also embraced by me.

3

I grew up in Lancaster, CA and lived with both my parents in an old, white house with a dark green trim. They paid $150 a month to rent this home. Even though it had two bedrooms, a livingroom and a kitchen, I knew our home was different. Our livingroom had all the typical items you might find in any livingroom: a nice, soft chair, a coffeetable, an endtable, a nick nack rack, a couple lamps. However, the twin size bed, clothesline, toy chests, and stacks of old newspapers (that Momma swore she would read) all cluttered the livingroom, forcing us to take a set pathway, as if balancing on a tightrope, to make it from one end of the livingroom to the other. Momma and I slept in the livingroom, while Daddy (whom I affectionately called "Da'y") slept in one of the bedrooms.

The other bedroom was a foreign place where I went when I felt like being adventurous. Piles of clothes and everything else that didn't fit in the livingroom were stored here. No one slept in this room, except for the mice. They left behind trails of doodoo pellets on the floor, on the bed, in the clothes. I used to stare at them from the livingroom as if I was watching television. The mice jumped in and out of my old shoes like they were celebrating Independence Day.

⸬

Saturdays in this house were simple, yet memorable. I woke up at 6:30 a.m., pulled back the curtain that separated the livingroom from the kitchen, poured a big bowl of Grapenuts, and sat down to watch the Snorks.

An hour later, I ate Momma's breakfast—Cream of Wheat with sausages. A half-hour later, Da'y woke up and cooked flapjacks, hot dogs, and fried potatoes with maple syrup poured on top—which I also ate.

Later on, I played with one of my dogs, Loni. I'd pretend we were at the beauty salon and pour mud all over her face to give her a mud facial. Since the mud was handy, I made a couple mud pies and mud muffins and let them bake in the sun. While they were baking, I went out to the garden to help Momma pick the radishes and corn. In between playing and picking vegetables, Da'y would give me lessons on how I should leave my shirts untucked.

Never calling me by name, he'd say, "Gal, ya see, city girls, they tuck their shirts in. You a country girl. You keep your shirt out."

I nodded and said, "Okay, Da'y," and hurried to play a little longer.

As a family, we spent late afternoons sitting on my father's worktable. Da'y would lay flat on his back, while he propped me up on his stomach. Momma climbed on the table on occasion, but most of the time she just leaned against it, resting her arm on Da'y or me…all of us laughing and watching the sunset, while our dogs ran around in circles, barking at us.

⊥⊥
⊤⊤

Momma was slightly heavy-set and appeared shy and sweet to the public, but possessed a fierce and loud spirit that only her friends and family (and maybe a few strangers) could testify to. Her almond eyes softly set in her round, fair-skinned face could gaze at you with affection if she was fond of you or burn through you if you tested her patience. She had a small mole at the base of her left cheek and dark black hair with streaks of gray. The wrinkles and calluses on her hands and feet could tell you how hard she worked as a homemaker and as a woman who separated onions at a local onion farm.

Momma was a gift giver. In one of my toy chests, she kept key chains and coffee mugs with people's first names on them; later I recognized those names as my father's children from his first marriage, Lou, Dana, and Jill. She kept them handy so she would have gifts for them just in case they might visit unexpectedly. When it came to favors friends did for her, she always gave them more than a thank you. Momma made sure she paid them back somehow, even if it meant secretly slipping them a $5 or a $10 bill.

Her life seemed to revolve around me and my activities. She was the woman who drove me to school concerts, tap dancing lessons, swimming lessons, diving lessons, roller skating competitions, and track meets. Momma was the one who broke toothpicks into tiny pieces and put them in my earlobes as temporary earrings so the piercing wouldn't close up. When she brought me to the latest movie, she made hot dogs wrapped in wax paper and smuggled them into the theater so she wouldn't have to spend extra money on food. On school nights, she cut up envelopes for my lunch money and carefully pasted them shut. With the little money she earned, she somehow saved enough for us to take trips to Disneyland and Magic Mountain or to watch the Harlem Globetrotters. She even saved enough money for me to go to Vancouver and Washington D.C. with the California Junior Scholastic Federation. This woman spent nearly every moment with me and spent nearly every penny on me. She never told me that she loved me. But I knew she did.

╬

Da'y was tall, confident, and friendly. He had a swing in his walk and a touch of grease in his hair. Da'y had smooth, dark brown skin with a carefully groomed mustache. He possessed an attractive smile and a strong handshake that warmed introductions and won over strangers. He often hid his eighth grade education by often using "sophisticated" words like "evidently."

When he encountered other Black men, he often smiled, nodded his head, and said, "How you doin'?"

The other men would say, "Aright. Aright," or sometimes, just gave a simple nod of acknowledgement.

Holding Da'y's hand, I asked, "Da'y, who's that? Do you know him?"

He looked down at me and said, "No, dear." I was confused, trying to understand why he would say hi to a man he didn't know and probably would never see again. But I didn't ask. We just kept walking.

Da'y was a hard worker. He did construction work in Antelope Valley, and arrived at the Union Hall by 6:00 a.m. every morning to see if there was work. Back then, as long as he showed up for roll-call everyday, his name would move closer and closer to the top of the list; those who reached the top were sent out to the next construction site that needed workers. Sometimes Da'y didn't have work, but most of the time he did. I was too young to know exactly what type of construction work he did; I just knew that with the sweat and dust above his brow, he'd come home from a long day, darker than the day before, with dirt beneath his fingernails and an exhausted sigh in his breath. I could see the glimmer of his gold filling as I always did when I saw him smile at Momma and I when he came home.

During the summer, he traveled to Marysville to do construction work, sending money home every two weeks. I used to hate it when he left because this meant no one could rescue me from Momma's temper when I got in trouble.

Although I had a lot of fun with Momma, she was the disciplinarian. Therefore, there was only so much fun I could have with her. With Da'y, every moment was fun, no matter how simple or mundane. Da'y was the "vacation" parent—the quick break away from the time I spent with Momma.

Early on the weekends, Da'y would jog to the garbage dump about 4 miles away and carry me on his back for the whole trip. The world seemed different so high up in the air. When we came home, he'd take a shower, and put baby powder in his underwear to freshen up. As soon as I knew he was finished, I ran into the bathroom and snapped the elastic in his draws just to watch the cloud of smoke come out. Later, we tended to the sunflowers, okra, corn, and radishes in his garden. When I helped him water the vegetables, he showed me how to put the hose in an apple juice bottle and let the water fan out to reach several rows of crops at a time. I spent hours staring at the water shoot out of the jar, forming tiny deltas in the dirt.

At night, Da'y watched the 6:00 p.m. news on CBS, which seemed to be interesting to everyone but me. I stayed quiet as I listened to Momma and Da'y yelling at the TV screen, "Reagan must be crazy!!" or "What's wrong with that Jarvis?!" And when it was all over, Da'y returned to his newspaper, then eventually went to bed. Before going to sleep, he'd always go to the bathroom first, and this excited me because I knew what would happen next.

He came out of the bathroom, walking toward Momma and I. He looked different. His lips seemed to have disappeared. Immediately, I began to laugh and I couldn't stop myself. With his mouth sunken in, he said, "Come here and gimme some sugar." The words rolled from his tongue and lips, not because he was sleepy, but because he had just taken his "choppers" out and all you could see were his gums.

"Come here and gimme some of that brown sugar," Momma would say as they embraced and kissed each other goodnight.

I jumped in the middle and onto Da'y's back, "Me too, me too!"

"Ummwa!" he'd say as he gave me a big, wet kiss on the cheek. "Goodnight, Gal."

"Goodnight, Da'y."

╬

As an only child, I usually played by myself or with my dogs. In general, I became used to being by myself and always found things to do. I rode my bike around the desert. Spent hours hanging upside down from the metal pipes that held up our clothesline. Made mud pies, and put dirt in my hair just because I liked the way it felt. When I went skating, I often kept myself amused by making up stories about the people who skated past me, creating a dialogue as if they were characters in my own movie. When Momma started working for the onion farm, she drove me to Mariposa Elementary School at 6:30 in the morning and parked the car in the desert across the street from the school. Before she left, she'd say, "Make sure you stay down low. That way no one crazy will try to get you." I did what she told me. While I was waiting for school to start, I stayed down low in the back seat, singing songs to myself and playing with my Barbies.

Even though I enjoyed being alone, there were times when I did feel lonesome. Often, I wished for a sister or brother to play with and became reminded of Sharon. I begged my mother to have another child. All she said was, "No." Discussion over.

╬

In elementary school, I was extremely sensitive. If anyone was mean to me, I immediately cried. Like in the first grade, Maynard, a scruffy boy that nobody liked, was showing a group of kids his new "Simon Says" game. I stuck my head in to look and he pushed my face back and told me, "You can't look!" I was so angry, but didn't say anything. I just walked away crying. Luckily, a friend defended me and sat with me until my tears dried up.

Early that same year, I cried so hard I was sent home. I was in a new, unfamiliar class that seemed scary, and I was upset because I couldn't watch *Electric Company* since I didn't finish my classwork packet. I was brought to the office and the school nurse consoled me and called my parents to come pick me up. I tried crying the following day in hopes of being sent home again. The teacher told me to return to my seat.

It wasn't until later that I developed a tougher skin. The more I played with my friends, the rougher I became. Even though I liked being alone, I enjoyed the friends I made in class and on the playground, especially when playing handball, Double-Dutch, or breakdancing. I made friends with just about anybody as long as they weren't mean. My closest friends tended to be kids who did all their homework and were funny—friends like Scott, Alba, and Ricardo.

Scott and I were in the same 4th grade class with Mr. Hall. We were best friends for awhile. We ate lunch together in the cafeteria everyday. He gave me piggyback rides during recess. We had a ball being silly, crackin' jokes under our breath while trying to do our classwork. Most importantly, Scott was just as big a fan of Duran Duran as I was. Being the two, most devoted Duran Duran fans on the planet, we made sure we displayed our loyalty in every way possible. Scott understood why I owned Duran Duran buttons, posters, folders, and tapes, since he did the same thing. We stood in awe of each other's latest Duran Duran paraphernalia while also remembering to write to their fan club every chance we could get.

We had so much fun together, until one day during lunch, a girl yelled, "Do you guys like each other?"

A lump formed in my throat as embarrassment and anger rushed through my 9-year-old body. Scott stopped with a spoon still in his mouth. Having never considered such an idea, we both said, "No! We're just friends." However, the stigma of being asked the question in the middle of the school cafeteria scarred our friendship forever.

That was it. The piggyback rides stopped. The jokes during class stopped. We still shared our fanaticism for Duran Duran, exchanging tidbits of trivia once in awhile, but the innocence of our friendship was replaced with caution.

Alba, a girl I didn't like at first, became my "runnin' buddy" in the 5th grade. She was the first person I "told off" for being so mean to one of my friends. Somehow we made amends and became best friends. She was a tomboy just like me. Not only could I play on the monkey bars and the swings with Alba, but I could also dig up worms with her.

Once during recess, we found some nice, wet dirt and dug up at least ten worms and put them in an old Oil of Olay bottle I had in my pocket. The bell rang and we had no place to put them. So we took some paper towels, wrapped up the top and then wrapped up the entire bottle so our teacher didn't know what we were carrying. We sat down with the bundle of paper towels on top of our desks. Both of us were fiddlin' around with the bottle trying to make sure the worms wouldn't escape. We ended up unwrapping the paper towel when the bottle was upside-down and all the worms fell out. Oh, God! In a split second, before anyone could see, I scooped up all the worms from the table and into the paper towels. "Um, Ms. Trint, can I throw these away?!" I asked, out of breath.

"Ye…," I heard the teacher say and instantly, I rushed out the door into the girl's bathroom and dumped all the worms into the trash.

Then there was Ricardo. In Mr. Tinner's 6th grade class, I sat behind Ricardo. Both us were diligent as we worked on our social studies and math homework. We loved the same music and enjoyed each other's company. We always compared answers and joked around, as well. To shut each other up, we would flash the palm our hand in each other's face and say "Blot!" or some other silly word. Every Friday, Mr. Tinner let us listen to our music while we did our homework. Ricardo asked if he could play his Egyptian Lover tape. Ricardo and I got our math homework done so fast when we listened to "Egypt, Egypt," not realizing how strange it was to hear that tune, "There's a place in France, where the naked ladies dance…" played in the middle of the song.

On the playground, when "Egypt, Egypt" came on Ricardo cheered me on when he saw me breakdancing, battling the boys. I was the only B-girl at Mariposa Elementary School.

"Egypt, Egypt" was among the popular songs we heard on the playground while the boys and I were breakdancin.' Ricardo knew I was the only B-girl in the 5th and 6th grade and had no trouble battling boys. Someone always brought out his giant piece of cardboard; anyone who wanted to breakdance, did. Although I could never bust a headspin or a flare, my favorite moves were the centipede (a.k.a. the worm), the kneespin and the backspin, always ending my bit with a freeze. At this time, all I knew was that breakdancin' was the latest craze. I had no idea that it was originally called B-boying, nor did I know that it was just one of the elements of a greater culture—Hip Hop. Around this time, I started hearing other songs besides "Egypt, Egypt" like, "Roxanne, Roxanne" by UTFO, "Planet Rock" by Afrika Bambaataa and the Soulsonic Force, "The Show" by Doug E. Fresh and Slick Rick, and "Friends" by Whodini, always having the urge to rub the ribbed side of my radio trying to imitate the sound of a DJ scratchin.' Back then, I couldn't tell you the titles of the songs, not even the artists for that matter, but I did recognize that these songs and breakdancin' felt connected and somehow it seemed like something new was happening.

My mother, though not entirely sure what was going on, was completely open to seeing me breakdance. After I begged her a million times, we even watched *Breakin'* and *Beat Street* together. When we passed Montgomery Ward, she didn't hesitate to pull over when I asked if we could get one of their old refrigerator boxes from behind the store so I could have something to practice on. Once we brought it home, she watched me practice my new moves with my maroon parachute pants and wristbands on, always getting ready for the next battle. Even though she knew little about B-boying, she always supported me.

During elementary school, Momma encouraged me to be involved in just about every activity imaginable. In kindergarten, I was enrolled in tap dancing classes. I hated it. The instructor was so strict she made me cry. So, Momma signed me up for a few other activities: swimming, diving, rollerskating. Of the three, rollerskating required most of my attention during elementary school and junior high. At the age of 6, I learned how to rollerskate and later in elementary and junior high, I started competing on the local and regional levels. Within a few years, I won a number of trophies in figures, dance, and freestyle—the three categories in competitive rollerskating. Even though Momma didn't make that much money, she somehow was able to pay for the monthly club dues, rollerskates, and the many dresses I had to wear for the competitions.

A typical night before a competition was extremely hectic. I wasn't nervous, just anxious. We both polished my skates and made sure every black mark was invisible. Momma taught me how to take a permanent marker and darken the heel of the skate to make my skates look brand new. She packed food for the following day and then did my hair. Momma sat me down between her legs, brushing out my hair using Johnson and Johnson's Detangler. She pulled and tugged, parting my hair down the middle and in the front with the pointed end of her comb, trying to get the lines as straight as possible.

Then she said, "Have I told you the story of how Filipinos were created?"

"No," I said.

"Well, you see, everyone in the world was bread dough. And God put aaaallll of us in the oven. He took some of bread out too early...those were white people.

Then there were some that were left in too long…those were Black people. And then there were those that were taken out at just the right time…and those were Filipinos."

I smiled thinking how nice it was that Filipinos were just the right color, but I later wondered why Da'y was burnt.

Momma finished parting my hair and wiped scalp moisturizer down the parts and any other area she could get to through my thick head of hair. Every now and then, she would take time just to feel the tiny waves that lay close to my scalp. "Oh, look it this! It's so wavy. Can you feel this?" she would say guiding my fingers through the waves. "It feels so nice—like ripples. Do you feel it?" she'd say again.

"Yeah," not realizing that Momma, whether she knew it or not, was teaching me how to love my hair. As my head throbbed, I used to wonder why my whole head of hair wasn't that wavy, or why I wasn't born with Momma's hair instead of Daddy's. Even though I liked feeling these waves, the rest of my hair (that wasn't so close to the scalp) still reminded me that I didn't have "good," straight, easy-to-comb hair like most of the girls at school. Despite my mother's love for my waves, my self-loathing began then and the longing for long, straight hair became an unattainable dream. By draping a long towel over my head and flipping it over my shoulders, I could pretend I had long, straight, beautiful, black hair. My misguided daydream was interrupted by a clump of that blue Bergamot hair grease scooped from the jar, the one Momma always called *pomed* or *pomada*. She rubbed it into her hands and into each section of hair. Each side was pulled into two braided pigtails held together with barrettes. My bangs were placed into rollers, so in the morning it would be nicely curled. The evening's work was done.

Mom woke me up at 2:00 a.m., sometimes 3:00 a.m. for the competitions, so we could leave the house by 4:00 a.m. After Mom uncurled my hair and put ribbons in it, we gathered the food, my skates, dress, nylons, and make-up and left. We had to carpool with someone else and travel 1 ½ to 2 hours to get to the rollerskating rink early enough for registration.

I had already finished doing figures and dance. Five minutes before doing my freestyle routine, I finally became nervous and could think of nothing but how badly I needed to use the restroom. "I want all of this to be over," I thought, "so we can go to some restaurant afterward," as we always did, "and then go home."

Mom was there to calm me down or scold me for being so nervous. She was just as nervous as I was the minute it was my turn to perform.

"And now, Number 213, Janet Stickmonnnnn," the M.C. announced. The audience applauded. I rolled out to the floor, head up, smiling, arms stretched out, chest up. All eyes were on me. I took my position on the floor and waited. The music began.

I did my footwork combination with no mistakes; my first jump, with a clean landing; my next jump came, and I fell. I could see my mother banging her head against one of the pillars near the floor. Confidence shaken, I finished my routine. I smiled, head up, arms out, pretending as if the fall never happened. When I left the floor I knew Mom was disappointed with my performance, as was I. I looked at her. She smiled and hugged me, not saying a word.

⌗

Around the time I learned how to rollerskate, I also entered my first spelling bee. From the 3rd through 5th grade, I placed in the top three at my elementary school. At the same time, I learned to play the flute and discovered my ability to sprint and do the standing broad jump. As my skill and desire to compete in spelling bees diminished, I developed an interest in speech contests and started competing in the 4th grade. I found that I liked speech contests much more than spelling bees. The problem was trying to convince Momma that I was better suited for speech contests.

One evening in the 4th grade, Momma was helping me study for the Mariposa Spelling Bee. "*Wield*. They *wield* power over their subjects. *Wield*," Momma said.

Spelling out the word on the palm of my hand, I began to spell the word aloud, "*Wield*. W-I-E-L-D. *Wield*."

"Correct," Momma would say and then continue to the next word on the three-page list. We repeated this process with every word. Halfway into the list, I misspelled at least ten words.

"You know, you need to study your words everyday," she lectured me. "And look up the definition in the dictionary. You know, Tara does that. She looks up words she doesn't know, and that's how she learns to spell so many words correctly. You should do that. You never practice your words. You never look in the dictionary for new words to spell. You should be like Tara."

Tara was the oldest daughter of one of Mom's closest friends, Auntie Estelita. I knew her well since we often played together. But with each time I practiced spelling with Momma, I began to hate Tara more and more. Hearing her finally say, "You should be like…" whirled me into a fit, and I yelled as if I was ready for a spanking, "I don't want to be like Tara!! I don't like spelling bees! Why do you keep comparing me to her? I'm not like her! I want to do speech contests!!"

And there I stood. I said it. I felt like I had just spoken on behalf of all my fellow elementary school brethren around the world…all those who have been held captive by their parents' dreams. After this brief, grandiose sensation passed, I found myself stock-still with my mouth half open, surprised at the words that just left my mouth. My eyes honed in on her every move, waiting for her to pull the belt out from under her pillow, where she always hid it. Then, I felt a calm sweep come over my scrawny body, even though I knew deep down I was about to get a whoopin.'

My mother stood there stunned, but looked as if she understood. "Okay," she said, "You like speech contests. Okay. You'll do speech contests then." I think Momma realized how much pressure she was putting on me. I won Momma's respect that night. Also in that moment, I defined my independence for the first time.

In the 4th grade I entered my first speech contest and won. For the next five years, I won more speech contests, while still getting straight A's and staying active in band, track, and rollerskating. In all of these areas, I was an overachiever and a perfectionist. At the time, speech contests seemed like one more thing I was good at.

Though unable to fully articulate it as a child, speech contests seemed more practical to me than spelling bees did. It would be dishonest to say that I knew exactly what effect speech contests would have on me—that I knew they would help me be more assertive; that I was developing a skill that even adults feared; that I wanted to prove I had a loud, clear, intelligent voice, even though I was usually quiet; that I rendered myself visible as I commanded the attention of my listeners. And yet, over time, competing in speech contests influenced me in each of these ways.

Indeed, entering speech contests was my choice; however, I believe Momma laid down a foundation. Getting me involved in so many activities sent an implicit message that there was nothing I couldn't do. Even though, I'll never know my mother's complete intentions for encouraging me to be so active, I do know that she wanted me to be successful in everything I chose to undertake. Because of her, I learned that I had many capabilities and more importantly, I had options. Without discovering at a young age that I could excel in so many areas, I may not have realized or become confident in my talents. And perhaps without knowing these talents, I would not be prepared for what was to come.

4

The livingroom smelled like smoke and damp wood. The adobe lining the walls covered everything in the house preventing me from distinguishing the bed from the coffeetable. The bottom tape deck of my radio was open. A piece of mud sat on the eject button. My clothes were spread across the floor--wet and brown. A layer of black soot covered the mirror of the nick nack rack and the trophies that stood inside. The pillow and blankets, draped with mud. Nothing was burnt in the livingroom, but when I walked past the kitchen and into the hallway, the smell of smoke grew stronger and I looked up and saw the open sky. The bedrooms and the bathroom were charred, especially Daddy's room. The firemen later told us that faulty wiring, as if gnawed by rats, caused an explosion near Da'y's room, and the fire ate its way through the rest of the house.

I didn't recognize our home. It seemed like a dream that we ever lived there. Just the evening before, Momma and I sat on the bed teasing Da'y about the Grecian Formula in his hair that was beginning to ooze down the sides of his cheeks, making thick, runny sideburns. We laughed so hard our stomachs hurt; Da'y ignored our taunts and continued reading his paper. It was difficult to fathom the place where we laughed had become smothered by ashes and mud.

We walked the house in disbelief, rummaging through clothes, newspapers, pans, toys, scared to discover what was destroyed and what was left behind. We salvaged almost everything in the livingroom and the kitchen, but nearly all of Da'y's belongings were destroyed. Of the clothes we saved, it took months to wash out the stench of smoke. No matter how much we tried to forget the fire, the tangled scent of Tide and cinder on our backs reminded us what happened that summer.

For the next month we stayed with our neighbor, Ms. Lynn, until her warm, hospitable smiles turned into tolerant, pursed lips. Momma asked Da'y, "So how long will we stay here?"

"Forever," Da'y replied without hesitation.

"We can't live here forever," Momma said, "We need to find another place to stay."

⚓

The radio was on and I was singing "Walk Like An Egyptian" with the Bangles. Momma stood at one end of our room near the bathroom. Da'y sat at the edge of the bed with his face in his hands.

"Why? Why us? Why? I've worked so hard," Da'y moaned. And he wept; he wept with his whole body. His cry came from deep within as if he'd been holding it in since the fire. Face still in his hands, he sat slumped over, still asking, "Why?"

I jumped on the bed and knelt behind him, holding his shoulder, stroking his back. Momma came up behind me and held his other shoulder and did the same. I'd never witnessed my father cry before. Since this was the first time, the moment seemed to tell me how hopeless our situation was.

The three of us were living in what seemed like a garage turned into a bedroom. It had no windows and felt worse than living in a motel room. It belonged to a portly woman named Devora who was an acquaintance of Auntie Lucrecia, a dear friend of my mother. Momma was reluctant to stay at this woman's home since she already knew what she was like. But we were desperate.

Devora was a bitter woman in her forties who rarely left the house and always smelled like unwashed vagina packed with rotten shrimp. Devora, usually found with a scowl on her face, behaved the way she smelled. Recalling a time when Devora asked me, "Do you really need glasses or do you just wear them to look smart?" I can say that everything that left her mouth was at best, crass and at worst, malicious.

One morning, the three of us were sitting in Devora's kitchen. Momma took out some food from the refrigerator that she planned to cook, and Devora began yelling and cussing at her for it. A battle ensued and Momma screamed back, until she finally dumped her body in the chair and laid her head down on the table, weeping, hiding her face in her arms.

"Oh, boy! Now she's crying," Devora said. "Fermon, why don't you just slap her?!"

"No! I can't do that!" Da'y said. And then silence. Da'y sat still and waited.

I watched Momma, feeling the weight behind her cry, thinking, "God, first Da'y, now Momma." As she raised her head, her wet, black hair covered her face. She pulled her hair back and I saw her—eyes swollen, face red. At that moment, having lived there for about two weeks, the three of us made the unspoken decision to leave this place.

My parents reached their breaking point at Devora's house. I had never seen both of them cry. I was the only one who hadn't cried yet and wondered when I would break down. After seeing Da'y cry, I already knew we hit rock bottom; but now that Momma cried too, we must have sunken below rock bottom—some irrecoverable depth. I, too, was beginning to wonder if things could ever get better for us.

There was an empty house up the street from where we once lived on East Avenue G. We moved in and were excited for awhile until we discovered the plumbing didn't work. During the weeks we spent there, we peed and buried our shit in the backyard. Harry Oleander, our neighbor's friend, came by the house a couple times each week to bring us fresh eggs. He heard about our troubles and told us about the extra trailer he had behind his home.

Harry and his wife, Minnie, owned a plot of land out on 80th Street East. After driving down a long dirt road, past tumbleweeds, Joshua trees, and maybe one or two homes every mile or so, we found their house. We slowly drove our loaded truck through the gate trying not to hit the chickens that were running out of the way. The old, raggedy trailer sat behind their house next to a chicken coop and a cage full of cramped pigeons. As we opened the trailer door, we immediately stepped into the kitchen; then five more steps: a small bedroom and a bathroom; two more steps: a slightly larger bedroom which became my room.

It was our fourth time moving and school hadn't started yet. We stayed here for at least three months and made this little trailer our home. It became the place where I taught my father how to write a resumé before I knew what a resumé was and the place where I fell in love with and eventually buried Amis Jewels, one of the kittens found beneath the house that burnt down. This was the place where I watched hens running away from roosters right before they got pounced and where Momma tripped and fell, still holding a saucer of cut tomatoes, undisturbed.

And this was where I listened to Bill Cosby's "Himself" tape, laughing myself to sleep to keep from

"No, we haven't seen him. I'm sorry," the officers said. One picked up the phone and informed the officers on duty about my father. "We'll keep an eye out for him."

"Thank you!" I said, running out the door, toward Spring Street, still scanning every face that passed. Across the street, about 100 feet away, near Auntie Pacita's shop, I saw Momma. She was waiting at the crosswalk, arm-in-arm with Da'y.

As they crossed the street, I jumped in the middle of the crosswalk and hugged him, tears streaming down my face. Curious strangers gathered around trying to find out what happened.

"Where did you find him Ma?"

"He was standing in front of McDonald's just lookin' around," she said.

"I'm so glad you're okay! I'm glad Momma found you!!" I said to Da'y.

"Okay," he said, seeming surprised by how happy we were to see him, not knowing he was lost. The three of us walked back to Auntie's shop holding each other. Perhaps, Momma already knew this, but as we walked up the stairs I realized that from this point on, at least one of us had to be with him at all times.

╬

Dad's Social Security checks weren't enough to live on, and Momma needed a stable job, so she enrolled in a clerical training program in Pacoima. Before she left every morning, she prepared Da'y's food and his pillbox so he would know what pills to take daily. My job was to help him bathe and get out of the tub without hurting himself, and not to mention make sure he didn't wet his soiled underwear in the tub—something he was notorious for.

Overall, Momma tried being understanding, but I watched Momma's frustration overcome her. With every wet, soiled underwear, every pill that fell out of Da'y's shirt pocket, every phone message he forgot, her blood boiled. Da'y's senility marked the advent of a series of never-ending arguments between he and my mother. Her only respite seemed to be watching the Johnny Carson Show. She scribbled Johnny's jokes on the bottom of tissue boxes, so in the morning, she could tell me what he said. We shared jokes for breakfast, so her evening dose of solace could spill over into the next day. But, her sadness never disappeared.

I don't think Momma expected to live this way in the United States. She didn't expect us to live in an old house that would eventually burn down or to be married to a husband who would become more like her patient than her companion. She didn't think she'd bounce from one job to another and depend on the government for bricks of cheese and butter and the local thrift shop for free bags of expired food. She may not have expected any of this, but she did whatever she could to take care of Da'y and I.

⌗

I knew we didn't have much, so it didn't take much convincing when Momma asked me to help her pick cans at the park to earn a little extra money. We started when I was in the 8th grade. On Saturday and Sunday nights, we filled the car with plastic grocery bags, clothespins, garbage bags, a milk jug filled with water, and a cart. At around 6:30 p.m., we set out for the Lancaster City Park in Momma's red Ford. As we pulled in and saw the hundreds of people on the baseball field, the basketball court, and at the picnic tables, I immediately felt Momma's excitement over the prospect of the thousands of cans that filled the trash.

Momma slipped on her yellow latex gloves and put on her scarf and jacket.   I put on my gloves and then lined the cart with a garbage bag and attached it with clothespins. Two plastic grocery bags were pinned to the outside of the cart to carry glass bottles. Like a warrior, Momma grabbed a 6-foot long stick that she used for picking cans from the bottom of the trash. We were finally ready—I, with the cart and Momma, with her stick.

We both sifted through wet pornography and shit-filled diapers to get to our aluminum treasure. Seeing cans at the top of the trash gave us hope that there were more at the bottom, so we turned the trash cans over to see what we could find.

When we were lucky, Momma would tell me, "Make sure you use the stick to get those cans out, so you don't fall in."

"Okay," I'd say, carefully putting the stick in the mouth of the can and pulling it out.

If we weren't lucky enough to find cans, then at least we found half-eaten hot dogs and ribs. We put these in a separate bag because we knew our dog, Loni, would eat them.   Every now and then, we found full cans of beer or Pepsi that we kept for later.

Picking cans was fun, even noble. I knew most kids my age would be too embarrassed to be seen picking cans. However, I took great pride in plunging my hands in the trash, no matter who was around.

"Momma," I said, "I'm glad I'm picking cans. I'm not embarrassed. At least I'm not spoiled. When I have kids, I'm going to have them pick cans, too—as long as it means we'll get a little extra money." Momma smiled.

My euphoria wore thin as puberty set in and I began to see kids from school at the park. I was a little more ashamed and more reluctant to pick cans when I saw my friends having picnics with their families.

"Mom, can we go to the park later at night. That way my friends can't see us?" I asked.

"No! Then we won't have as much time to pick cans." For awhile, she insisted we leave around 6:30 p.m. However, with each weekend that came, I pleaded and argued with her, until eventually we were leaving at 10 p.m. and returning home at 1:00 a.m. or 2:00 a.m. I became less enthusiastic about picking cans, especially when I noticed people who didn't respect our work (or us) as much as we did.

Mom and I were near the bleachers between the baseball field and the snack bar. A baseball player came walking from the field with a can in his hand, finishing off the last few drops of soda. Mom walked toward him and asked, "Are you throwing that away?"

He said, "No! Go back where you came from!!"

Mom yelled, "What?!! Why don't you go back where *you* came from? I'm only asking for your can! Why don't you go back where you came from? Go back to Russia or Germany or wherever you came from!!!!" And she chased him down with her stick, her eyes piercing through him, lips tightened, teeth gritted, ready to stab him. He quickly walked away, mumbling something under his breath, finally throwing his can in the trash.

I wondered who else besides that baseball player viewed my mother as a stranger invading their land. Later, I knew my mother was swallowing her pride to dig in trash— that her dignity was sacrificed far more than mine. If we had the choice, we probably wouldn't spend our weekends crushing our dignity in the park and redeeming it for a few dollars each week. And yet, this money was one of the few things we could count on.

5

My freshman year in high school, I decided to join the youth group at Sacred Heart Church. As a child, I took catechism classes and attended Mass every Sunday at this church. When I walked up the stairs to my first youth group meeting, I could remember all the nights Momma sat in the back seat of her car, wrapped in a blanket and holding a thermos of canned corn, waiting until my catechism classes were over.

The summer after my sophomore year, I went to a weekend retreat with the youth group at a Benedictine monastery. We sang songs, performed skits, prayed and learned things about each other that we never knew through our weekly meetings.

When we returned to Sacred Heart, Mom wasn't there to pick me up.

I called home, "Mom, we just got back. Can you pick me up?"

"Okay, I'm on my way."

When she arrived, she hadn't been feeling well. Within a couple of days, Mom caught the flu and spent days lying down on the couch, while Da'y stared at the television.

Mom got up and walked across the livingroom when all of a sudden her knees gave out, and she was left kneeling on the floor. She laughed, "Ha! Look at me. I just fell. My knees just gave out."

"What happened?" I asked.

"I don't know," she said, "My knees just gave out. And now I'm on the floor." I helped her up, and she walked back to the couch. For the next few days, I didn't think anything of it, until her flu became worse. She was extremely weak and had a fever that lasted days. Her knee was hurting and her fever persisted. I tried exercising her knee a little, slowly bending it back and forth—my version of physical therapy.

"*Aray*!! Ohh. Okay," she moaned. Then she looked at me and said, "You know, you'll make a good physical therapist when you grow up." I smiled.

As each week progressed, she became weaker. Mom could barely get up to use the bathroom. Da'y and I helped her, until she was no longer strong enough to get up, even with our help. We placed an old coffee can next to the couch, so she didn't have far to travel to use the bathroom. Da'y wasn't alert enough to fully understand what was happening. As for me, I became the head of household, cooking dinner for the family, making sure Da'y bathed and took his pills. After dinner one night, Momma asked me to take some pills out of her purse. I had no idea she was taking medication. When I found the bottles, I noticed the label on one of them read, "Gastro…" I didn't know exactly what it meant, but it was a hint that Mom had been having stomach problems and never told me. As I handed her the pills, I wondered how long she'd been taking them.

Mom asked me to go to the hospital supply store downtown to buy some crutches so she could get around the house. I walked from our apartment and slightly past Sierra Highway, about a 40-minute walk. At fifteen, I'd never walked into a store by myself before and didn't know exactly how to ask for what Mom needed. Being very formal, I said, "Excuse me. My mother is having trouble walking and needs to buy some crutches."

The woman behind the counter looked down at me and said sweetly, "Well, I'm afraid we only rent them out. But I'll bring a pair out to you anyway." She walked to the storage room in the back and brought out the crutches.

"You can adjust them by pressing these buttons," she said as I watched the crutches get shorter and taller.

I walked back with the crutches in hand, hoping they would help Mom. They worked for maybe a day, since she was too weak to stand. I returned and traded the crutches for a wheelchair, but it was too wide to fit through the hallway, so I returned it, as well.

After about three weeks, Mom and I decided to go to the emergency room at Lancaster Community Hospital. Even though she was in pain, she forced herself to drive while I sat in the passenger's seat. We waited in the emergency room for at least a couple hours before she was helped. When the doctor finally examined her, he found that her knee was severely bruised and prescribed some Tylenol painkillers.

A week had passed and she wasn't improving. She moaned and cried in the middle of the night. I sometimes woke up hearing her moan, but didn't know what I could do. She asked me to call Dr. Rahi, her physician. After trying to contact him several times, I was finally able to schedule an appointment. When Dr. Rahi saw her, his examination didn't take long. He said, "She's jaundiced. There is a problem. She needs to be admitted into the hospital."

Mom was immediately admitted into Antelope Valley Hospital. As she lay in her hospital bed, she said, "I'm so happy I'm finally in the hospital. It's a relief. Maybe someone could tell me what's wrong with me."

"Yeah, everything is alright now. You'll be alright," I said as I held her hand.

By Friday, she was transferred to a room in the Coronary Care Unit. This section was secured, so I had to use the phone outside to let the nurses know I came to see my mother. The door opened and the nurses directed me to her room. It smelled stale and sterile. When I walked in, there were tubes in her nose and an I.V. attached to her arm. I was later told that she was diagnosed with liver cirrhosis, kidney failure, and multiple bleeding ulcers. The doctors explained to me that the liver controls the clotting factors in the body and since her liver wasn't healthy, her bruised knee was far too much for the liver to handle.

I often visited her by myself and stayed with her all day and most of the night. Occasionally, I brought Da'y with me, but most of the time I left him at home partly because I knew he couldn't manage being in a hospital all day and partly because it would take too long to get him ready each morning. When I arrived, the nurses allowed me to come in before visiting hours and stay as late as I wanted. I didn't want her to be alone. And I didn't want to be alone.

╬

Momma was always thirsty, but the nurses told me not to give her water. They gave me pink sponge swabs that I could dip in water to temporarily relieve the dryness in her mouth. I gently wiped the saliva and blood from her lips with the wet swabs and left a freshly soaked swab in her mouth that she sucked on like a lollipop.

That weekend, one of the doctors recommended a line be placed through her chest near her collarbone connecting to her liver. I didn't understand exactly what the line would accomplish, but the doctor assured me that it would help her condition. Since Da'y wasn't fully coherent, I gave my consent.

By Tuesday, she seemed to have more energy. Seeing her speak and smile gave me hope. We watched television, as I stroked her hand. A detergent commercial that I wanted to show her came on TV. A child wearing a bright-colored shirt was happily playing a cello that seemed twice his size. When Momma saw the commercial, she began to laugh. It was good to see her laugh again.

Some time passed and we were still watching TV. She turned to me and said "You know, I won't even see you graduate from high school."

"No, don't say that. You'll be at my graduation. You'll be up there with all the rest of the parents, rootin' for all their children. You'll be there. Don't say that." I tried to reassure her that she wasn't going to die.

She tried her best to look as if she believed me. She just smiled and softly said, "Yes."

She was trying to prepare me for the worst. Her death was imminent. And somehow she knew. I looked out the window that day, thinking about what might happen if Momma died. "I guess I would stay with Auntie Estelita," I thought, imagining myself riding on the swings and playing games with Auntie Estelita's four children. But the thought wasn't consoling. I promised God, I'd never be bad again as long as He let Momma live. I pictured us walking in the parking lot from Kmart and Mervyn's to the car, as we always did when she was healthy. I thought to myself, "I am 15 years old. There is no way Mom is going to die. Da'y is old and can't take care of himself. I would have to take care of him on my own. And try to go to school. If Mom died, I would have to do all of this. And live without her. This won't happen. These things only happen on television." My mind continued racing. These thoughts that seemed to keep me from getting too depressed, did nothing but exhaust me. It was getting late, and I already ate some of Mom's peas since she wasn't hungry and I was. It was time to go home.

╬

Da'y sat in his usual chair in front of the television. He looked at me and said hello, but never asked about Mom. He didn't remember that Mom was in the hospital, even if he visited her the day before. I couldn't begin to explain to him how she was doing because he wouldn't understand. I just fixed him some Top Ramen, gave him his pills, and let him go to sleep.

I tried eating, and then visited the neighbors upstairs to let them know how Mom was. I returned to our apartment and waited for *Arsenio Hall* to come on. I stayed up late watching *Arsenio* to avoid being alone with my thoughts. The later I stayed up watching his show, the less time I spent worrying at night and the less likely I'd wake up worrying the following morning. *Arsenio* kept me sane and relaxed. I laughed, laughed so hard I forgot Mom was dying. But, when *Arsenio* was over, I stopped laughing, and reality flooded in. I had to go to sleep. And worry. And tremble. Despite my efforts, I woke up at 5:00 or 6:00 a.m. with my heart racing, "Is Momma going to die? Will she live? Oh, God please let her stay alive. I promise I'll be good. I'll never do anything bad, again. Promise. Oh, God, I promise."

I dragged my body out of bed, feeling my pillow already wet with tears. I had a headache and was nauseous. I tried eating some cereal, only to vomit right after. The fear of losing Momma was tangled with the uncomfortable state of uncertainty making it difficult to know what made me more upset.

Before leaving for the hospital, I promised Momma I'd bring her a copy of a money order paid to Household Insurance and her Lord of Pardon prayer book. I found the money order, but I couldn't find her Lord of Pardon, so I brought another prayer book instead. When I left, I kissed Da'y goodbye and rode the bus to the hospital.

Momma was weaker than before. I came in and put her prayer book and a rosary beneath her pillow. She didn't seem to notice. She was less alert and a little delirious. By Thursday night, she was much worse.

Fr. Eller, the pastor of Sacred Heart, prayed and anointed her. She kept scrambling around, trying to get out of bed.

"I have to go. I have to go now," she said, still squirming.

"Where are you going to go? Your knee is swollen. You can't walk," I tried reminding her, practically holding her down.

"I want to go home. I have to go. I want to go home," she said.

By Friday, she was in a semicoma. Her eyes were half-open. One eye was a little crossed.

"Why is her eye crossed?" I asked the nurse.

"It's the toxins in her system," the nurse said. "You see, there are toxins given off by the liver and the kidneys." She then showed me a chart, pointing out two different columns, "These are all the toxins a kidney dialysis machine can eliminate and these are all the toxins that are emitted by the liver." I noticed her liver released the majority of the toxins. "Even though using a kidney dialysis machine will help a little, it won't be enough to eliminate all the toxins." Though I was thankful for the explanation, it didn't make me feel any better.

╬

Saturday, Mom was in a coma. She didn't speak. That morning Uncle Godo, Auntie Pacita, and their youngest daughter, Anabelle, came to visit my mother. They wept when they saw her. One by one, they touched her face and hands. We stood around her bed just looking at her. I gazed out the window and saw swings and Auntie Estelita's children. Fr. Eller was now praying over Momma. After a little time passed, our relatives left. Then Fr. Eller left. I stayed at the hospital past visiting hours, and then finally went home. Momma never woke up from her coma that day.

Sunday morning, I returned to the hospital and brought Da'y with me. Da'y just sat in the chair looking out the window or watching television. He didn't quite know what was happening. I sat next to Mom; she was still in a coma. I looked out the window again and saw the swings. I looked back at Mom and her eyes began to open slightly and a couple of labored breaths left her lungs.

"Nurse! Nurse!" I called, "What's happening?"

She looked at my mother and said, "She's dying."

I quickly grabbed her left hand and stroked it, telling Da'y to do the same. He quickly grabbed my mother's right hand and gently rubbed it. I heard Momma deeply inhale. A final breath left her body as her chest sank. Her eyes opened wider. I heard the flatline beep of the heart monitor. The nurse reached for it and slowly turned the volume down. Then she gently closed Momma's eyes.

It was 12:15 p.m., Sunday, July 16, 1989.

Every Sunday, my parents and I attended the 11:00 a.m. Mass at Sacred Heart Church. Momma waited until Mass was over before dying. Meanwhile, Auntie Estelita was at the laundromat when she had a sudden rush of memories of my mother. She felt my mother was near. It didn't occur to her until later that Momma was saying her goodbyes.

I didn't cry right away. I walked into the hospital chapel in disbelief, and sat down in the reclining chair. I cried a little, but not much. The room smelled clean and new. The sun shined through the stained glass window, casting hazy yellow, red, and blue light on the cream carpet. A box of tissue sat on a short table near the entrance. I was glad it was there, but wondered if I'd need it. Peering at the shapes and colors in the window, I knelt down before it and prayed, asking God what should happen next, still thinking it strange that I wasn't weeping uncontrollably. Though I didn't want to lose her, I was relieved when she died. A huge part of the anxiety rested in the uncertainty of whether she would live or die. The wondering was over. She was dead. So, what was I supposed to do next?

It was understood that if Mom died, I would stay with Auntie Estelita. I assumed Da'y would be staying with us. However, Estelita said that one of Mom's last requests was to have him admitted into a nursing home so I wouldn't have to take care of him and go to school.

When I woke up the next morning, I wasn't nervous and nauseous anymore. I walked into the bathroom and stared in the mirror. I imagined I was speaking to Mom, "I love you Momma. I miss you. I know you are still here with me. I'll continue to work hard, with a smile." Then, I began to cry.

That day I called friends and relatives to tell them the news. Within a day, my half-brother and sisters, Lou,

Dana, and Jill, came down to help with the burial arrangements. My mother's friends, Auntie Cristita and Auntie Estelita were also there to offer their support. We went to Halser-O'Reilly Funeral Parlor where we had to make arrangements for the funeral service.

Sitting at a table with adults discussing Mom's funeral was surreal. I was doubled over in my seat with my head under the table. I felt a nudge on my shoulder telling me to sit up. When I did, I saw Da'y sitting next to me, looking less alert than I.

Once the plans were finalized and we agreed to cremate the body, we were led downstairs to see Momma. It seemed like we walked into a cavern. The air was cold. The room was dark with the exception of the sun that acted as a spotlight cast upon Momma. Her naked body lay covered by a sheet of plastic and a charcoal gray blanket. She looked refreshed. Healthier than she looked in the hospital. There was no stress in her forehead and no tension in her brow. When in the hospital her hair was matted, she laid on that table with it brushed out and flowing toward the floor with frost glimmering between the strands. As I noticed the frost on her brow, I touched her body to see if the rest was still frozen. Her right thigh was rigid. She was there, but she wasn't. Auntie Cristita helped Da'y walk toward Momma. He said nothing. He looked at her and turned away nearly collapsing.

Within the next couple of days, Lou, Dana, Jill and I drove to the Department of Social Services and the Social Security office to see if our Dad was eligible for long-term care. When we arrived at the Social Security office, Lou began to explain the situation; then Dana tried. When they realized that I was the only one with all the information, they let me speak. I rattled off a string of sentences that would soon become the tape I'd play when someone would ask about my family, "My mother died, my father is 77 and we've been living on my father's Social Security checks for a few years now." I watched the gentleman behind the counter, as well as, Lou and Dana listen attentively.

The man smiled and said, "I'm really impressed. You are very aware and articulate for being 15." Lou and Dana nodded. I didn't think that what I said or how I said it was that big of a deal. I thought I was supposed to be clear when I spoke to a person in any government office.

The man continued, "Mr. Stickmon is eligible for long-term care in a nursing home. Given the circumstances, he won't be placed on a waiting list. You," as he looked at me, "are eligible for a lump sum payment of $200 as a result of your mother's death." He then gave Dana the number to call regarding the lump sum and she handed it to me.

⚏

My brother and sisters brought me to Texas Cattle Company for lunch and gave me advice as to what I should do next. When the bill came, I did what Mom would have done and reached into my purse to help pay for my share. Dana said, "No! That's okay. We'll take care of it. Don't take your money out too quickly when people do something for you. It's not good." Embarrassed, I quickly put the money back into my purse and accepted the free lunch. This wasn't very easy for me, and I'd find that this wouldn't be the last time I'd have difficulty accepting gifts.

We began our search for nursing homes by starting with one on the west side of Lancaster. It seemed like an old motel with a large cafeteria. I couldn't see Da'y being happy there, so we moved on. The next one smelled like rotten eggs. The residents in their beds looked lifeless. Those who still had strength in their legs, walked without purpose, without destination, brushing the perimeter of the hallways as they held tightly to the rails. We passed by the activity room where people were watching television, playing cards, and playing with puzzles. Whatever kept them occupied seemed to only maintain their motor functions, but nothing else. They passed cards and bingo chips like photos of people they didn't know. They had boredom and disappointment in common. Just a phone call would have been enough for some of them to regain the color in their flesh. Instead, they stared out the window, watching random people pass by. The nursing home saddened me, but it was better than what we saw earlier. All four of us agreed to admit our father into this facility.

I didn't want Da'y to look like an old man. When my siblings and I shopped for him, I made sure he had his favorite caps and colorful shirts, so he would look young and cool. We bought him plenty of socks, underwear, shirts, and slacks, making sure all of his belongings had his name on them. I pictured him, walking with that swing of his, looking sharp and smooth, walking with a purpose, even if he was just going from the kitchen to the bathroom. I didn't want him to lose that in the nursing home. I didn't want him to be as old and hopeless as the other residents there.

6

On Daddy's first day in the nursing home, he walked in with his old, tattered suitcase carrying everything he owned. I helped him to his room, and stayed with him the whole day.

Da'y was still an active man—far more active than the rest of the residents in the nursing home. Once we placed his bag in his room and unpacked, we were on the go. I refused to allow him to wither into someone who watched the walls of his bedroom all day. I walked him around the nursing home to remind him where everything was—the dining room, the television room, the recreation room. We were bookin' it down the hallway; Da'y was lookin' smooth with his brown cap and his trademark swing. We passed everyone up. I was proud. "My Daddy is young!" I said. Then, I was quickly reminded of his age when he complained, "My ass hurt!!" We stopped, rested, then started up again, only slower than before. I brought Da'y to the recreation room and learned that he liked ping-pong. His coordination surpassed all the other residents. I even had difficulty keeping up.

I left the room for a moment and spoke with one of the directors of the nursing home. Her arm was deformed and I tried paying attention to what she was saying, but kept looking at her arm. The thought of leaving my father alone at this nursing home combined with the look of that woman's arm, made me nervous.

"I don't want to leave my Dad here," I said, tears streaming down my face.

"Now, everything will be okay," she said with a warm, sweet voice, "We'll take good care of your father."

We'd never been separated before. I didn't want to leave him in this place with 100 other elderly people. And once I would leave him, our shared memories of home would end. I began remembering riding his back to the garbage dump and snapping the elastic in his underwear; remembering how he used to say, "John Brown!!" if something fell down, or surprised him, or say "Da's a whoopin' boy, right there!!" if someone told him unbelievable news; he was the man who fed me and carried me. And now, I was feeding and carrying him.

I held his face, crying, "I have to leave you here tonight. But I'll be back tomorrow."

"Okay," he said.

⚓

Often when I visited him, I caught him sitting in front of the television. On this particular Sunday, it was no different. It was lunchtime. I took him out of his room and brought him to the dining hall. We sat down, and he asked, "Where's your Momma?"

Disappointed, yet not surprised, I reminded him, "Momma died, remember? Remember, she was really sick."

"Ohh," he said, as he held his forehead, ready to cry, "When did this happen?"

"She died July 16th, remember?"

Every time I came to visit, he asked me where she was, and I watched him relive the news of her death each time: him grabbing his forehead; the look of confusion on his face; him shaking his head in disbelief; tears welling up in his eyes.

His tray was placed before him. He tried eating his mashed potatoes, but kept missing his food, placing an empty spoon in his mouth. I fed him, like he and Mom fed me. And when he was done, I played the flute for him and the others in the dining hall. They applauded and I returned to my seat across from Da'y and fed him spoonfuls of peach cobbler. I spent the afternoon with him walking around and telling him stories. He listened intently.

When I promised I'd visit him everyday, there was no doubt in my mind that I would. But slowly my visits went from everyday, to once a week, to once every two weeks, to once a month. Pretty soon I only visited him only during holidays and summers. It was these intermittent visits he waited for.

7

Once I finished carving clover patterns into the potato, I dipped it into lavender paint. Firmly pressing it against the wall, I created a border near the ceiling, adding a nice touch to the bedroom. Tara and Serena, Auntie Estelita's two daughters, also pressed their lavender potatoes into the wall. Auntie Estelita bought a bunk bed that I would share with Serena. As we prepared the bedroom, all three of us were excited to share the room together, and I was happy to actually have new siblings who were around my age; Tara was 17 and Serena was 14. Auntie Estelita also had two sons, Albert who was 15 and Kent who was 16, who shared the other bedroom.

The Poncé family—Auntie Estelita, her husband, Valentino, their four children, and Lolo (the children's grandfather)—lived in an old two-bedroom house with a broken water heater. The house was near Palmdale and was bordered by a dirt road on one side and the Mojave Desert on the other.

I was excited to live with all the children and they were excited to have a new addition to the family. We laughed and played, told stories and cracked jokes together, not forgetting to also do our household chores. Lolo always told me stories and explained to me the meaning of "by and by": "You know, like in a song, you sing, 'I have not seen you…by and by.' It means I have not seen you por a long time. Yeah." All of us would tumble in laughter, unsure if we were laughing because we loved his Filipino accent so much or because of the high level of importance this 80 year old man placed on the phrase.

A couple weeks had passed. It was that time of year for the annual Antelope Valley Alfalfa Festival and Fair—popularly known by the locals as "The Fair." I entered my first major pen and ink drawing into the fair to see if I'd win a prize.

My best friend, Deanna, and I went to "The Fair" together. We had become extremely close while my mother was in the hospital. Our mothers were good friends, as well. Every time there was a parade or a concert our school band performed in, our mothers stood side-by-side watching us play our flutes. They shared a special camaraderie that neither one of us completely understood. Perhaps their immigrant backgrounds brought them together—my mother being Filipino and her mother being Japanese and each of them married to American men. That made both Deanna and I products of interracial marriages. I imagine they shared quite a bit in common in the same way we did.

Deanna and I walked around the park and then to the art exhibit. I couldn't wait to see if my piece won a prize. We walked up and down the aisles, admiring all the artwork and also searching for my drawing. And there it was…with a third place ribbon on it.

"Man! I'm gonna tell Momma," I thought. But I forgot. I couldn't.

Deanna and I stopped at one of the concert areas. We sat and talked for what seemed like hours.

"I really miss my mom. I don't know how I can be without her. What's going to happen to me?" I said.

"Janet, you'll be alright," she said, "Your mom will never leave you. She'll always be by your side." I believed her and replayed those words in my head. She wrapped her arms around me and gave me a long, warm hug as I wept. We then walked to one of the vendors selling corn on the cob. And our evening ended, taking big bites of corn doused in butter, the way Mom and I always ended our trips to the fair.

╫

One morning, I woke up and stared out the window. Through the translucent drapes, I could see the plants outside, sitting on shelves. The sun pushed its rays between the plants, casting a dreamlike image of paradise onto the drapes. There were white pillars standing freely in a lawn that stretched for miles. White blossoms were in the trees and a few fell to the ground. Taking a deep breath, I could almost smell the sweet air of paradise. Its beauty comforted me. It was a sign. Momma was in heaven now. I didn't have to worry.

╫

On the first day of my junior year, I carefully studied my friends' faces attempting to detect undesired pity. I smiled and went to class, did my homework—business as usual. I tried hard to keep myself from crying and tried my best to continue getting straight A's. Hearing Mom's voice say, "Continue living with a smile," kept me going. That's what I did. I smiled so often that I fooled everyone—including myself.

That year for U.S. History, I had the same teacher I had my sophomore year for World History—Mr. Shepardson. Somehow, he heard that my mother died. At the end of class, he called me up to his podium. "I'd like to tell you I'm sorry to hear about your mother," he said, "Who are you living with now?"

"I'm temporarily staying with the Poncés. You know Tara and Kent Poncé, right?"

"Yes, yes I do. Well, I'd been thinking. You know, my wife and I, we can take care of you. We can be your guardians," Mr. Shepardson said.

I was deeply touched and surprised by his offer. "Well, thank you," I said politely, not knowing exactly how to respond when a teacher opens up his home to you, "For right now, I'm staying with the Poncés. I might be staying with another one of my aunts…my mother's half sister. You know, Filipinos stick together!" I said proudly smiling. "But thank you, though."

I walked out the door still surprised by the whole thing. "He really cares about me," I thought.

8

I was beginning to doubt if I'd ever become a true part of the Poncé family. I had only lived with them for two months, and I still enjoyed being with Auntie Estelita, Lolo, and all the kids. However, Auntie's husband, Valentino, always found fault with me. From the moment I moved in, I knew something was wrong because he barely talked to me. I ignored it at first, until his irritation with me became more obvious. For instance, when I told him I couldn't ride the bus to and from school, he said, "Why can't you ride the bus like everybody else?"

"Well, I have band practice before school. And after school, I know I'll need to go to the library."

He said something under his breath that I ignored, and the conversation was over. Later Auntie Estelita decided to take me to school early in the morning, but after school I had to take the bus since no one could pick me up. This was reasonable. Besides, it wasn't urgent for me to be at the library anyway. With her, she was willing to find a solution, whereas, Valentino seemed uncompromising. I got the impression that it was fine for me to live with his family, as long as I wasn't too much of an inconvenience.

A few days later, I took out some sausage to cook during lunch, not realizing there was already a meat dish for all of us to eat. Valentino said, "Hey, what's the matter? The food we have here isn't enough for you?"

"No, it's enough. I, I didn't know," I said, sheepishly putting it back in the refrigerator.

I had to watch my every move when he was around; nothing I did or said was ever right. His attitude always reminded me I was an outsider and needed to be careful not to take up too much space.

⁜

Sitting on the bed in the livingroom, I looked at the digital clock. Its numbers looked like red devil eyes staring at me. Across the room were the drapes of paradise. I sat with these images juxtaposed as I contemplated whether or not to stay with the Poncés. For some reason, my mother's half sister decided she didn't want to take care of me. However, my Auntie Pacita and Uncle Godo wanted me to come live with them. As I thought about Valentino, my decision was made.

⁜

Auntie Pacita had called me several times since Mom died, asking me to come stay with her and the family.

"Jinit, come stay with us, ha. We are your pamily," she'd say.

"No, Auntie, it's okay. I'll be okay here," I always said.

This time I called her. As I waited for her to pick up the phone, I looked at the red eyes of the digital clock staring back at me.

"Hello, Auntie? It's me Janet." My voice began to shake as I started to cry, "You know how you've been asking me to stay with you? Well, is it still okay? Can I come live with you?"

"Yes, yes, you can lib with us," she said with excitement in her voice, "Do you lub me?"

"Yes, I love you, Auntie."

"Jinit, I and your Uncle Godo will come pick you up Saturday."

"Okay, Auntie. I love you. Thank you."

They came as promised, driving from El Monte, a little over an hour away, in a pink and maroon minivan. Three of their children, Anabelle (who was 18), Remi, (who was about 20), and JunJun (who was around 30), came along. We loaded the van and I said my goodbyes to the Poncés. Then we drove to my new home.

Being with another family was awkward for me, having just finished trying to adjust to the Poncés. When I moved in, I became the youngest in the family. Everyone spoke English, but for the most part *Visaya* was spoken at home. Uncle Godo always sounded angry when he spoke *Visaya*, so I avoided him. Auntie Pacita was always asking me questions. Every time I opened my mouth, a "Why?" or a "What do you mean?" or a "How are you now?" would immediately follow. I asked Anabelle, "Why does your mom always ask me so many questions?"

"I don't know," she said, "She's just interested in you, that's all."

I looked around their home and could remember how many times our family came to visit them. Mom first brought me here when I was 12. Back then, Anabelle and I became instant friends; we used to play with our Barbies together; I taught her how to *freak*; she taught me how to make "Toad in a Hole"--grilled toast with a fried egg in the center; she'd beg my mother to let me go to the movies with her when Mom always said no. And we had just visited them a few months before when Da'y got lost near Auntie's sewing shop in Downtown Los Angeles.

That was April. A lot has changed in five months. I was back in their house again. Only this time, I was alone, and I wasn't visiting.

⌐⌐

Every day in this house I felt numb, never entirely present. I went to bed exhausted from being confused and depressed all day, kneeling against the bed, praying.   I prayed because I had nothing else. Everything had been pulled out from under me. Mom was gone. Dad was away in a nursing home. Loni was given to the dog pound. And I had moved away from all my friends. I had no choice but to surrender to the one thing I had left—God.

"Lord God, I pray. Please guide me. I don't know what to do.   Momma why did you leave me? If you hadn't left, I wouldn't feel like this. Da'y wouldn't have to be in a nursing home. I wouldn't have to move in with a family I barely know and have to transfer to a different school. God, what am I supposed to do?" I begged, pounding the edge of the bed.

Then I thought mid-prayer, "I do have a bed. I do have people that actually want to take care of me. Thank you, God. Please, just guide me. I love you. In the name of the Father, Son, and the Holy Spirit. Amen."

As I crawled into bed, I imagined God and I standing face to face.   Without hesitation, I punched Him. Then I hugged Him—not out of remorse but because this best conveyed the complexity of what I was feeling. After getting comfortable beneath the blankets, I thought, "What kind of dysfunctional shit is that!!"   And when I told Anabelle what I was thinking, she felt the same way.

I tried to get into Los Altos High School, a predominantly white school, with a reputation for offering a better education than most schools in the area. However, I decided not to lie about my address in order to get in. By the end of October, I enrolled at Rosemead High School.

This school was gray, and most of the classrooms were found in one main building, much different from Antelope Valley High. I walked into the registration office, filled out some paperwork, and then saw a guidance counselor. I began to cry in her office.

"Why are you crying, Janet?" the counselor asked.

"I don't know, I just..." but I did know. I just couldn't begin to explain.

She stopped asking questions, but still looked concerned as she tried figuring out my schedule. My classes were chosen: Trigonometry, English, French III, Chemistry, Marching Band, and Typing.

For the next three months, I woke up every morning crying, hating everything about life and worrying that I'd never get into college because my grades weren't as high as before. I didn't put much energy into getting dressed for school, simply because I didn't care how I looked. Everyday, I put on a wrinkled T-shirt, acid-washed jeans, and sneakers. Once I pulled my hair into a ponytail and put on my large, maroon glasses, I threw on my oversized jean jacket, and I was ready.

Anabelle drove me to school and I told her how worried I was about college.

"I don't think I'll ever get in. I'm not getting A's like I used to. Trig is not making any sense and I'm barely getting a B- in Chemistry," I said, sulking in the passenger seat.

She looked at me weird. "You'll get into college," she said, sounding annoyed. "Why are you so upset over just a couple of bad grades?"

"I don't know," I said, looking out the window. "She obviously doesn't understand," I thought, "I have to get straight A's. It's my only way to get into a college of my choice." Given that I hadn't received a B since junior high, not getting straight A's was devastating. And since everything else was breaking to pieces, I had to make sure that at least my grades didn't slip. Otherwise, I could see my future falling apart, too.

╬

I wandered from class to class like a zombie, never feeling so depressed in my life. I had nothing. On top of that, I had no one at home to confide in. In Trig class, I sat in the first row, 4th seat back. It took everything within me to keep from crying in front of everyone. Sometimes, I laid my head down on the desk until lecture started. My tears fell all over my desk, making a mess that dripped alongside the edge. The next class was English. I did the same thing, resting my head on the desk until it was time to pay attention. Once my desk was wiped off, I sat up and began taking notes.

Ms. Wilkes, my English teacher, never got up from behind her desk. The woman was about 80 years old. With a sweet, feeble voice she'd say, "Okay, class, your homework for today will be to define all the words written on the chalkboard and write sentences for them, as well." This was the routine everyday in class. She would tell us what the class work or homework assignment would be, and we did it. Never once did we actually see her write anything on the board; words just miraculously appeared before we entered the classroom. And though I was grateful, I did find it strange that she never assigned books for us to read.

At lunch, I ate by myself. I walked around the campus trying to find a place to sit, but every bench and table was taken. I decided to sit in the little grass area between the library and the main building. At first I faced the hallway, since that's what everyone else did when they ate their lunch there. However, watching everyone pass by laughing and cracking jokes became unbearable. I turned away and faced the gray wall of the main building. I opened up my lunch bag. I sucked in my tears between bites of my sandwich and took short sips of my juice, just sitting there—me, the gray wall, and the muddy patch that separated us.

I really don't know what kept me from killing myself. My incessant cries weren't always for my mother. I was crying over everything that had happened to me. I was alone even while in the presence of others; I tried to ignore what I lost by blanketing my pain with fake smiles. I was forced into adulthood. Planning Mom's funeral, figuring out where her insurance papers were, going to the Social Security office to make sure Da'y received his Social Security benefits while in the nursing home, waiting in four different lines at the Department of Social Services to fill out over ten pages of government forms, and eventually repeating my story to a different social worker every couple of months, all forced me to be an adult. These things weren't supposed to be my responsibility. This wasn't supposed to happen to me.

⚏

Walking up and down the school corridors, I began to notice the number of students of different ethnicities, even though I was still one of the few Black students at that school. When I walked to class, I thought, "I've never heard so many people speaking Spanish and Japanese before," assuming that they, or their families, must have been from either Mexico or Japan. I was fascinated, but also disturbed. When I spoke to my friends back in Lancaster, I told them that I "lost my innocence" and now noticed race.   I missed not noticing it, and yet I couldn't understand why I had never noticed race before.

⊥⊤

I signed up for all the extracurricular activities I was involved in before Momma died. I signed up for the marching band; I continued making pen and ink drawings; when track season came around, I joined the team. I didn't try very hard to find friends. But, through band rehearsals, track practices, and class projects, I slowly began to make friends. I didn't do anything special; I only put my best effort into everything and minded my own business.   I didn't realize that this would attract even more new friends.

Michele and Kelly, Anabelle's former classmates, were members of the band.   When they discovered I was Anabelle's cousin, they invited me to hang out with them during lunch.   After a couple lunches together, they said, "You know, after you came to the first couple after school practices, we were impressed. And then we saw you rolling your feet as you marched and we wondered where you'd come from.   We were wondering why you were so dedicated," they laughed.

Then there was Joe and Carlo who were on the track team and also in the band.   Joe played the saxophone and Carlo played the trombone. They were both funny and fairly popular with the girls at school, especially Joe. When track season began, the three of us became friends. They noticed I was good at the long and triple jump; I noticed they were good polevaulters.   All of us were in band together, and we were all a little crazy. Becoming buddies seemed only natural.

With each month that passed, I felt better about being at a new school since I finally made friends and was getting the A's I wanted. My high school life was turning around.

Unfortunately, my life at home wasn't. There was no one at home I could really talk to. I couldn't run home to tell my parents what happened at school that day or to tell them that I made new friends. I couldn't tell them that I hated English class or that my group in French III was going to perform the *Three Little Pigs*. And I didn't see my parents in the auditorium or the bleachers during my band concerts and track meets. I didn't have them anymore. And none of my relatives showed up to any of these events. I thought my new family could take my parents' place. Instead, I had an aunt and uncle who worked over ten hours a day and were too exhausted to attend anything I did.

As far as my cousins were concerned, I could tell they had a problem with me. Often Remi, the cousin who always called me "four eyes," snapped at me, demanding that I wipe the table or wash the dishes after dinner. Anabelle, did the same, reminding me with a threatening voice, "Be ready to clean the house on Saturdays." Her attitude surprised me since we used to be really close as children. JunJun was nice, but usually indifferent. Besides the Poncés, I never grew up in a household larger than three people—my mother, father, and I—so, having people other than my aunt and uncle, the authority figures of the house, take the liberty to extend their control over me was difficult to get used to. Not only did I have to adjust to everyone, but I also had to grow accustomed to what was expected of me; I learned quickly depending on how angry or bossy Anabelle or Remi sounded. Granted, I wasn't the cleanest person in the world, so learning to clean the table and wash the dishes after every meal was a good habit to form. However, they were often rude and loud when they wanted my help. Daily, I wished they used a kinder approach. While wiping the table, I replayed in my head how I would ask someone to help around the house. "Can you help me wipe the table please," I'd say smiling, "Thank you." I kept hoping they would be polite to me and treat me with some respect.

I told Auntie Pacita that they, particularly, Anabelle, were being mean to me, not expecting her to tell Anabelle or anyone else in the family. But, when she did, Anabelle yelled at me again. Soon, I discovered that everyone in the house knew what I had said. Another lesson learned: there's no such thing as confidentiality in a large family. As a result, I decided to keep all my thoughts and feelings quiet and trust no one in the house.

I stepped softly in their house and said little to my cousins. Every night after dinner, I wiped the table and washed (or dried) the dishes. I then went into my aunt and uncle's bedroom to watch *The Cosby Show* by myself—my only constant source of laughter. Later, I went into Anabelle's room, closed the door behind me, and did homework.

I did everything to avoid being yelled at. If I was going out or if I had to stay late after school, I always told my aunt and uncle; and if they weren't home, I left a note. I made sure I helped clean the house. I even found myself cleaning out my kinky hair from the tub after a shower, even when I frequently saw my cousins' long, straight, black hair everywhere.

Despite all this, at least one of my cousins, at any given time, found fault with me. Remi accused me of being greedy for not sharing my shampoo and conditioner with the rest of the family, failing to understand that the texture of my hair required special care. When she saw me studying, she always said, "Wow, what a nerds!" never noticing her mispronunciation. Another cousin, Lita, who was in her thirties and lived with her husband in San Diego, decided to lecture me after coming home at 11:00 p.m. one night from a football game that our school band had to play for. She claimed that I told no one, when in actuality I did.

According to one of my cousins, I was getting away with a lot more than they did. Translation: I was always out all the time. They obviously didn't understand the difference between being out partying and being at a legitimate, extracurricular school function. To my knowledge, it was never an issue for Auntie Pacita.

Once, the family was sitting at the kitchen table, and we heard the refrigerator making strange noises. Auntie Pacita said, "Seeee! It's your mother, Jinit. She says your going out too much." I was angry that Mom's spirit was used in such a way, but I was also frustrated that my family was under the impression that I was out partying, not being responsible. No one could truly appreciate that I was a smart 16-year-old who earned good grades, participated in school activities, and never missed Sunday Mass. I received little to no encouragement for anything I did (with the exception of Auntie Pacita). The only time I heard a cousin say anything that remotely resembled a compliment was Lita saying, "Oh, when you get rich, don't porget us, ha," or saying, "Jinit, don't porget to pray for me, ha!" when I was on my way to Sunday Mass.

I missed the encouragement my parents gave me. I couldn't rely on my new family for it. Besides, I could tell Remi, Anabelle, and Lita couldn't even stand having me around.

⌗

When I came home from school, I took a break to watch cartoons before I did my homework. Uncle Godo (who I later called Tatay) and I watched *Chip & Dale* and *Tale Spin* together. Tatay and I laughed so hard watching Chip and Dale run around trying to stay out of trouble. Holding my stomach with tears rolling down my face, I tried to catch my breath after laughing at Tatay's jokes and watching him crack up at parts of the cartoon that I didn't think were funny at first, until I heard him laugh. There was something endearing about a 60-year-old man, unwinding from work by watching cartoons and having the absolute time of his life, laughing so hard until his phlegm-filled cough stopped him.

Tatay was special. After thinking he was always angry when I first moved in, Anabelle convinced me that that was just the way he spoke. I discovered he was the jokester of the family--the playful one.

Tatay threw on his favorite record by Yoyoy, a popular Cebuano singer and comedian, and sang along, "I love my country, Philippines. I love my country. I love my country Philippines, my Philippines. I will not stay away from here, I will not leave here. Because I love my country Philippines." As he sang with Yoyoy, Tatay stood in the middle of the livingroom dancing—his hands were balled up into fists and he'd bob them close to his body. When the time was right, one fist shot out while kicking out one of his legs to the side. I always waited for that kick to the side to send me into a fit of laughter. It tickled me every time.

Tatay teased me all the time, pointing at the roaches in the house, "Hoy, Your priends. Your priends are here. Tell your priends to go home, ha," and he'd laugh so hard with his mouth wide open, showing all his rotten teeth, so pleased with his joke.

Auntie Pacita was the gentle one. She had a heart that forgave the transgressions of any human being regardless of whether or not they apologized or corrected their failing. Auntie would always tell me at the dinner table, "You are like our daughter, ha. We lub you. Okay, so that's enough, you hab to eat." As she put rice on my plate, she would give me advice with a thick *Waray* accent, "Bepore you *sanduk* de rice, you hab to make de sign ob de cross on it, ha. Por good luck. And don't stack your plates until eberyone at de table is pinished. Por good luck. Oh, do you hab a boypriend, Jinit?"

"No," I said.

"Oh, good. You're too young. You pirst, you pirst, you hab to complete your estudies and den when you pinish your course, den you can hab a boypriend. You can get married. And have a big house, ha."

When we were alone she told me stories the way my mother did, "You know, during the Japanese war, I almost got captured. I was just a little girl. I was walking up de mountain with a bag of rice on my back. And when I got to de top ob de hill, dere was a Japanese soldier, dere. I said, hello in Japanese. Then he asked me to count in Japanese and I did. And he let me go!"

Tatay and Mama (what I eventually called Auntie Pacita) made me feel like their daughter. The two of them gave me so much, far more than just food and a home. They loved me and gave what time and energy they could, in spite of the ten-hour days they worked and the full house of adult children they already had.

Interestingly enough, they always found a reason to celebrate even though they didn't have much extra money. It could have been someone's birthday or baptism or no reason at all, and there would be a party. You could tell people the party started at one time and guests arrived at least 2 or 3 hours early.

For instance, for one of Auntie Pacita's birthday parties, a few people began to arrive at 1:00 p.m. The party was supposed to begin at 3:00 p.m., but nearly everyone was there early—some came to help, while others just came to get the party started.

Uncle Roy, Tatay's close friend, immediately drew our attention, pretending to be Elvis as he played his guitar. Nang Taling, a family friend who worked at Auntie's sewing shop, was sitting at the table chopping carrots into thin slices for the *lumpia*. Anabelle and I called Nang Taling "Heh?" because we thought she was *bungol* since all she ever said to us was, "Heh?" Nang Heh? always laughed the loudest at all of Tatay's jokes as she flirtatiously removed her glasses and fanned her knees in and out with each laugh.

Then, Nang Bebing came to the door; now the party could begin. With garish flair, Nang Bebing came in wearing her bright yellow stretch pants and her blouse with the giant sequined butterfly on the front. She was the woman who, without shame, told dirty jokes—the ones that everyone loved—the nasty jokes about all of her ex-husbands. She often spoke to me in *Tagalog* or sometimes *Cebuano*, forgetting that I couldn't understand either. I never stopped her though; I just listened, hoping I could understand at least some of the words.

The food was ready. I almost cried at the sight of it all on the table: *pancit* with slices of green onion on top, *lumpia* stacked on three different plates, chicken and pork *adobo* and a huge pot of rice with the *sanduk* spoon planted in the center.

We stacked food on our plates and ate. By the silence in the room, everyone knew how good the food was.

After eating, all of us danced to everything from Yoyoy's music to "Funkytown." Auntie Pacita took me by the hand and taught me the Cha-Cha. And once everyone was tired, we said goodbye to some of the guests, while others spent the night.

Little money, but many celebrations. The family escaped their troubles during these parties. And so did I. For a brief moment, I was part of the family.

⚟

During Mass, Anabelle was crying. She turned to me with her black hair wet and acne on her cheeks, saying, "I have to tell you something. I'm sorry. I'm sorry for being so mean to you. I was jealous of you. When you moved in, I was no longer the youngest one. You were the youngest one..."

I looked at her surprised. I never expected an apology. And besides, I could remember when she didn't like being the "baby" of the family. When we were children, she complained about how much she hated being called *Ta* or *Tata* (which is short for *bata*, meaning baby in *Visaya*). "Don't call me *Ta*! I'm Anabelle!" she'd always say. I guess there was still a part of her that still wanted to be the "baby" of the family.

Her anger toward me wasn't just my imagination. I was relieved when she admitted it. Her confession explained a lot. By moving in, I replaced her and received all the attention that she once had. I admired her honesty and took it as an invitation to rekindle the friendship we once shared as children.

⚟

Anabelle had a saucy, daring character with a slight flirtatious side. She was an outgoing, outspoken young woman who was very comfortable joking around with friends and very capable of drawing out even the stiffest person with her sense of humor. She wasn't a terribly great student and usually her time was taken up by graveyard shifts at Norm's Restaurant.

Within a month, Anabelle met one of the cooks at work named Gilberto. She showed up to work one day to pick up her check. She wasn't in uniform. Her wavy black hair hung to her shoulders and her red blazer and stretch pants demanded everyone's attention. People at work had never seen her like that—and neither had Gilberto. She won his attention instantly.

She became nicer and nicer to me as a result. I soon became the first person she shared all her secrets with, which was still strange since I was so used to her mean side. She told me all about her encounters with this man: his fear of approaching her, the note on a napkin he left on her car windshield, their late night talks. I listened, but kept asking, "Well, do you know his last name, yet? Find out his last name," not because it could reveal anything about him, but because I figured after a few dates, she should at least know the man's last name!

⊥⊤

It was quiet in the livingroom. The television wasn't on. The sun was setting and it was getting dark in the house. Anabelle and I sat on the couch. Something seemed wrong. She turned to face me and said, "I have something to tell you…I'm pregnant." Looking down, bawling and trembling she said, "I didn't know who else to tell. You're the first person to know."

"Oh, Anabelle. I promise. I won't tell anyone," I said, holding her, "This isn't something to cry about. You are going to bring a beautiful life into the world." I tried to make her feel better. However, I knew the wrath of Auntie Pacita and Tatay was imminent.

When she told her parents she was marrying Gilberto, she didn't tell them she was pregnant, even though Auntie Pacita suspected it. They were outraged; even her siblings were angry. They were partly upset because they believed she was too young and was throwing away her dreams of going to college and becoming a flight attendant; but mostly, they were upset because Gilberto was Mexican. Each member of the family took turns condemning her and filling her head with racist lies about Mexican men.

Anabelle was confused and didn't know where her life would lead her. She considered getting an abortion, but didn't. Gilberto ultimately convinced her to keep their child so they could raise it together.

Anabelle and Gilberto decided to get married in a chapel in Downtown Los Angeles. Anabelle wore a beautiful wedding gown that Auntie Pacita sewed for her and Gilberto wore a sharp, black suit. Only Auntie Pacita, Tatay, and I were there from Anabelle's side of the family. JunJun, Lita, and Remi insisted on teaching Anabelle a lesson; they all decided to "boycott" the wedding by going to Bingo instead, objecting to her marriage to a Mexican man.

I never took joy in seeing her fall victim to our family's malice, but knowing that someone else understood how cruel they could be comforted me.

9

I could hear Boys II Men singing "Let It Snow" and slowly the family, one by one, began to wake up. We opened our gifts, hugging and kissing each other. Friends and relatives stopped by throughout the day delivering gifts, eating, and catching up on the latest news. The cauldron of gumbo, Brenda's specialty, made with crab, chicken wings, corn, hot links, shrimp, and rice was bubbling on the stove—thick, hot, and ready. The homemade macaroni and cheese was being pulled out of the oven as the potato salad was pulled out of the refrigerator. Deviled eggs, green beans, mashed potatoes, stuffing, and a giant turkey added to the many dishes that had already blessed the kitchen. In the livingroom, the Seven-Up cake and the Red Velvet cake sat on a portable card table, tempting and teasing all who passed by. Laughter, love, and Jesus' presence mingled with the aromas, unmistakably marking this day as Christmas in the Stickmon house.

╬

My brother, Lou, worked for American Airlines. After Mom died, every Christmas (and sometimes Thanksgiving), Lou sent me a ticket to the Bay Area to visit his family, as well as, Mama Lila, his mother, and my two sisters, Dana and Jill. I was so excited to be with everyone, mostly because it gave me a chance to be with other Black people.

The moment I stepped in their car and in their home, I felt at home and yet also in a different world. A local R & B station was playing on the radio. I smelled the faint scent of hair grease, coconut lotion, and cigarette smoke. In the bathroom, a stack of Jet magazines sat on a rack; hair grease, a curling iron, a couple of kinky hairs were around the sink telling me I was in a familiar place. And as usual, Lou's joy filled the house as he joked around and teased everyone.

Lou inherited our father's friendliness, but had a much better sense of humor. On trips to the grocery store, cashiers knew him by name and Lou sparked up conversations with them, as well as, any random person in line. This made it difficult for me to distinguish a friend from a stranger. Whenever he teased someone or explained something, Lou's every word "tickled" me (as he'd say). Whether he was driving through East Oakland telling us, "Y'all better duck! The rough-ians live 'round here," or at home telling one of his sons, "Ya drink, smoke and ya gotta earring! That's three things wrong whicha!" he'd have me giggling all day.

I clung to his every word as if he'd just given me a toy to toss around. I became immersed in his mannerisms, his slang, the swing in his walk, the joy in his voice. As I picked up words and idioms reminding me of what I was too embarrassed to admit I was missing, I hoped to never be exposed as a phony, an imitator of Black culture, even though I was Black. I realized I was so used to being the only Black person in a crowd. As a result I learned to assimilate, being blind to the importance of my own Blackness. However, at Lou's house, I caught myself staring back and forth between the darkness of his hands and the fairness of mine, learning to love the Black skin and culture that was ours.

He didn't know it, but I admired him. Lou, who was protector, provider, jokester, and nurturer, represented all that was strong and gentle in my world. His life taught me that you didn't have to have a college education to be intelligent. It was his experiences—his knowledge through living—that I valued most. He was the one to tell me about McClymond's High School and the free breakfast program the Black Panther Party started there. He taught me what to be careful of and who to watch out for. As I listened to his stories, he also listened to mine. Whether on the phone or in-person, he was always concerned about what I ate that day, which was then followed by "So how's school?" Even when I went into far more detail than the average person might care to hear about, he still showed his interest by asking me more questions and relating it to something he already knew.

Mama Lila was another source of inspiration whose words, "You be a sweet girl, now hear?" helped me sleep at night. A woman in her 70's, Mama Lila carried herself like a woman half her age, vibrant, wearing one of her sharp dress suits with the matching church hat, walking with an elegance and a self-respect that made everyone think twice about stepping in her way. She was never overbearing, but was always aware that she possessed a wealth of experience that deserved recognition. Once she told me, "Oh yeah, I'll sit with the President and have a conversation. I don't care. There's nothing to be ashamed of."

She was a wise woman who knew more than any book could tell me about history or about life in general. She shared with me many stories from what she'd seen during the Civil Rights Movement to some of the reasons why she divorced my father. And I can't forget that she always showed an interest in my personal life.

Even though I was the child of her ex-husband's second wife, she always treated me as her own, showing me nothing but love and respect. She understood my inquisitive nature, and though I was well aware that she was much wiser and experienced than I, never once did I hear her say, "You're too young to understand." Because of this, as well as her wisdom, I was less feisty around her and never hesitated to take her advice.

╫

When I wasn't alone talking to Lou or Mama Lila, I was talking to Lou's daughter, Chera, who shared her room with me during my visits. We used to exchange secrets as if we were sisters; I occasionally talked with Lou's sons, Terrence and Chris, but we usually shared short conversations about school or the chocolate chip cookies and *lumpia* I made for them. Other times, they just joked around, calling me "Aunt Janet" or "A.J." being tickled by the fact that I was too young to be their aunt. And as far as Lou's wife, Brenda, we rarely spoke and when we did, we only engaged in polite conversation. I never felt as close to the rest of the family as I was to Lou. Although, I loved everyone very much, there seemed to be some barrier keeping the rest of the family at a distance.

As a family, they rarely shared the sorts of conversations that I was stimulated by. I was always eager to talk about life—about hopes, about death, about college plans and experiences, about future professions. I wanted someone to ask me how I was and if I missed my parents. I was interested in getting personal, in being heard, and in hearing their deepest dreams. I didn't hear these conversations take place. For the most part, I heard conversations about television, parties, music, or movies— things I knew very little about. Of course, there were also the funny stories or the intermittent teasing of anyone that just walked into the room. Aside from that, I didn't hear much of anything else. Perhaps, these conversations took place when I wasn't around. I don't know.

This is not to say that as a family they weren't close. There was no doubt that there was an unsaid bond they shared. They loved each other deeply and were quick to defend each other against anyone who might bring harm. It was a bond that I so desperately wanted to experience, but never fully did.

From morning 'til night, the television was on. The family was either watching a movie, a soap opera, a football game, basketball game, or BET. If the television wasn't on, then Terrence, Chris, and Chera were playing video games.

The brain deadening effects of the television and video games were taking hold. My legs felt a tingling numbness as I grew bored and groggy. Being taught that it was rude to complain when you're a guest in someone's house, I quietly grabbed a book from my backpack and tried to read even though the noise distracted me. Later, I convinced Chera to go jogging and rollerskating with me just so I could get out of the house.

An invisible barrier existed between Brenda and I, pushing me to the periphery of the family. Whenever I arrived, she was always polite to me and gave me a hug, but never seemed genuinely interested in me. She lacked the motivation to initiate a conversation, as if something about me made her uncomfortable. I felt like she found me to be a nuisance. I heard her complaints about me, sometimes about my suitcase being in the center of the room or about me being just like my mother when referring to how quiet I was or how repulsed I was by cigarette smoke. At first, I thought all of this was because I once criticized her church for not allowing women to wear pants; but as I thought about it, I noticed something was wrong between us long before that.

Sometimes I heard her criticizing other Black people. Some of these people carried themselves in a very sophisticated way, at least from my perspective. Some were educated, some liked to stay to themselves, and some could be considered by folks as "proper." When I overheard conversations or jokes being made, I might hear a comment like, "He's just different." I knew exactly what that meant. I tended to get along quite well with the types of people she criticized. I could only conclude that I was "just different" in the way the others were. Perhaps, I was seen as uppity because of my speech, my education, or maybe my apparent disconnectedness from mainstream Black culture at the time.

I wanted to be closer to her somehow, so I tried making conversation while she was watching *All My Children*, one of the soap operas I watched as a child. In hopes of prompting a dialogue, I mustered up some esoteric details about one of the characters. And sure enough, it worked. One of our longest conversations was about the different characters from *All My Children*. Though I was disappointed that all we could talk about was a soap opera, I settled for it, since at least we were speaking.

Even though nothing was ever made blatant, I could tell that some members of my family didn't view me as "Black enough." It was the way they looked at me whenever I spoke; the way Chris almost didn't let me talk to Lou on the phone because I sounded like a bill collector; it was the way they laughed at me when I told them I didn't know who Father MC was; it was the way they politely, smiled and nodded whenever I spoke about school. It was obvious that they had difficulty relating to me, as I had difficulty relating to them.

Perhaps, it was also my quiet demeanor that made me seem unapproachable. For the first few years of visiting them, I only spoke when spoken to, except when I was alone with Chera. I was quiet, introverted, and self-conscious. Constantly weighing what to say, what not to say, and how not to sound stupid. As a teenager, I didn't have the skills or the confidence to speak free of inhibitions, especially in front of other Black people; I was always worried that I wasn't "Black enough," whatever that meant. Having grown so comfortable with being alone, I didn't know how to express myself in small or big crowds, especially with a family that I just recently began spending time with.

As I grew older, I was still fairly reserved. Eventually, I began to speak more, but still about more serious issues and still only around those that I felt most comfortable with. I was analyzing and deconstructing my environment incessantly around family and wasn't always aware of when my criticisms became inappropriate or just plain annoying. Perhaps, all of this was what made me "just different." If I was perceived as uppity or standoffish, this was not my intention. I never meant to flex my intellect. Being an introvert and a critical thinker at a young age was just how I was.

Generally, I was uncomfortable with Lou's family as a whole and felt left out even after sparse attempts (mine and theirs) to initiate conversation. The tug between my desire to be close to them and not knowing how, was the source of much of my stuttering or sometimes my overly formal speech. Crippled by my awkwardness, I slipped further into that familiar silence—my comfortable, private, lethal solitude—escaping any reminder that I didn't belong—escaping any reminder of how alone I felt. Even among my own people, my own family, I knew the dull ache of invisibility.

In spite of the emotional distance I felt in their presence, the physical distance when I returned to Southern California hurt even more. I missed the laughter and the stories. And I missed being with other Black people.

With Auntie Pacita, Tatay, and my cousins, I tried recapturing what I missed by telling them the stories and jokes that were shared at Lou's house. They politely smiled and nodded, but didn't really understand. In my daily language, I used every bit of slang, and every expression I could remember, to desperately hold on to what I considered my Blackness. But I still felt disconnected since my speech was divorced from its source. This became a precursor to other attempts I made to reconcile my two backgrounds. The result being frustration.

╬

The 1991 Billboard Awards came on and En Vogue was accepting their award. When they stepped on stage they sang the introduction to "Hold On." I made sure I recorded it. Goose bumps ran along my arms, and my whole body rose with excitement. I wanted to share it with Auntie Pacita and the family.

"Auntie! Remi! Anabelle! Watch this video! It's En Vogue! It's amazing! You'll love it!" I called out to them.

They came into the livingroom. I pressed play. En Vogue sang. As I slowly turned to them, waiting to see if they would be as excited as I was, a burst of laughter hit me in the face. En Vogue wasn't even done singing! And I stopped the tape, furious!

"What are you laughing at?! What is so funny?!" I yelled.

They didn't have an explanation, they just made whooping and howling noises, mocking En Vogue's voices.

And I collapsed within myself and said nothing. Pissed and disappointed, I ejected the tape and ran to my room.

It was at that moment that I understood that Black people had been laughed at all our lives. We could reveal our deepest talent and be laughed at. My own family wasn't just laughing at what they heard on the video, but they were laughing at my people and the music my people created. They were laughing at my father. They were laughing at me.

After each trip I made to Lou's house during the holidays, I returned noticing more ways in which Blackness and darkness were demonized in my aunt and uncle's house. It surfaced in subtle and not so subtle ways. For example, there was a time when I had my hair relaxed, and I was sitting in the bedroom. Lita came in and said, "Wow! You're so pretty. You don't even look Black." This was coupled with comments made by another cousin like, "Wow, she's really pretty for being Black," when referring to Phylicia Rashad and other beautiful, Black female celebrities—as if being Black *and* pretty was some rare, unimaginable occurrence. When it came to dating, there was a premium placed on having white boyfriends. I noticed Auntie Pacita and Tatay were pleased when their daughters dated and later married white men, eventually deferring to the men's "American-ness" and "expertise" on life in the United States. One of the running jokes in the household referred to Anabelle's license plate: 3PWM763. Lita and Anabelle laughed, saying it stood for, "Three Pure White Men 7-6-3."

I didn't want to be accepted as a full-fledged Filipino, if it was gained at the expense of my Black side. The most distressing feeling in the world was not feeling at home in places that were supposed to be home. I was between races and between homes. Although the Black side of my family fully acknowledged my Filipino side and never insulted it, I still felt viewed as less Black, due to my speech, my light skin, my education, or my quiet nature. When I was with the Filipino side of my family, my Blackness was insulted and I became less Filipino because of that Blackness. I was without parents. And as far as I was concerned, I was without people who loved me completely, with the exception of a few. I had yet to find my home.

꜀꜀

The older I became, the more I understood why I missed not noticing race and why being with students of so many different ethnicities at Rosemead High felt so strange to me. I had transferred from a school, Antelope Valley High, where the majority of the students were white, and yet somehow passed through my mind as not having a race...somehow being *beyond* race; no one spoke of their whiteness; a person's race was only mentioned if they *weren't* white: that *Black* kid who sits behind me; that *Chinese* girl who raised her hand.

When I was at Rosemead High, the student body was for the most part Asian and Latino, with a few students who were Black. The majority of the teachers and a handful of the students were white. After being there for awhile, I learned that the people I initially called "Mexican" weren't just from Mexico but were from Nicaragua, El Salvador, Guatemala and many other countries within Latin America. And when I thought I was hearing Japanese, I was hearing Cantonese, Mandarin, and Vietnamese. There were more people from different backgrounds than I'd ever been exposed to.

Until moving to Rosemead, a part of me took great comfort in living the mindless bliss that told me race was never an issue for me, unknowingly granting white people the status of being absent of race—being just people. I resisted any mention of race because race was rarely mentioned; and if it was, it wasn't dealt with intelligently or respectfully. I could remember wanting to ignore my racial background; I subconsciously wanted to be white and went so far as to ask people to call me "Kelly," the last name of one of my best friends who was white. I learned to loathe my appearance because the boys I liked—white guys, usually blond and brunette with brown or blue eyes—didn't like me; but I hated myself even more so because I didn't look like the other girls—the popular white girls with the straight hair and straight noses who wore khakis with button down shirts.

I began to recall a time in elementary school when I was called a nigger and later separated myself from other Black kids that didn't "behave" because I didn't want to be judged based on their behavior. I ran home to my mother one day showing her the palms of my hands, saying "See Momma!! I'm not Black. I'm white, Momma, see." Even though I could tell she was mad, she didn't give me the whoopin' of my life. Instead, she explained to me what was true about my hands, my skin, my blood—that I was Black *and* Filipino. And then I remembered how she chased off the white baseball player at the park who told her to go back where she came from.

In junior high, I spewed out the few *Cebuano* words I knew, often telling my friends stories about Mom's family in the Philippines, explaining to them that the reason why I was a quiet person was because my mom was Filipino. I did all these things because it was a part of myself that wasn't so obvious. Since the average person saw me as Black, telling these stories and using *Cebuano* words made me feel more interesting and "exotic." Being mixed drew the attention and envy of many, and I knew it.

Somehow I told myself that I never dealt with race…when I had been dealing with it my entire childhood, subconsciously soaking in racist ideas about myself and other people of color, while becoming deluded into believing that noticing race at Rosemead High was a bad revelation.

AND YOU'LL NEVER KNOW I'M HERE

I have stumbled upon your space,
Where your bare feet trod,
Where the breath you breathe is your own.
Old wounds, worn-out dreams, modest, intermittent resurrections
All color my past
Bruises cloth my body.
May I still enter?

I promise not to wear the garb of a participant.
For one must create space for a participant
I'll just slip into the role of spectator,
Watching from the outside in,
Sitting at the edge of my seat,
Laughing with you,
Crying with you,
Wanting with you,
If I don't comprehend, I can't ask,
For I am a spectator,
So, I will reach out, and for a brief moment, I will be with you.
Living and loving the charade.
Wiping tears and sweat from my face,
Looking down and then seeing my seat,
My seat and the distance separating me from you.
The revelation sears my self-deception.

Pardon me.
I have forgotten that I am a spectator.
I will be in no one's way.
No abrupt motions. No graceful flourishes.
Only soft-spoken words that you will never hear
And you'll never know I'm here.

I will not ask for your attention.
For it takes energy to give attention.

Instead, I shall welcome numbness,
As I stand alone in a room of many,
A piercing loneliness more pronounced than one's own
solitude.
I will be in no one's way.
No cries. No complaints.
Only insincere smiles and seething indignance
And you'll never know I'm here.

I will not ask you to live this horror with me.
I will not ask you to touch my blood
Lest your routine be disturbed.
Instead, I will sit in a white chamber,
Nurturing the despair that invites my inadvertent suicide.
Never calling out,
Afraid of witnessing my lament fall to an irrecoverable
depth
A suffocating depth,
Where hope is swallowed by death,
Where grace cannot resuscitate the human will.
I will be in no one's way.
No footprints. No breath.
Only memories of a silhouette.
And you'll never know I'm here.

10

Mom's urn sat on Anabelle's dresser for almost a year. I gazed at the gold tin box, speaking to her everyday, "Hi Mom. How are you? Me? Things are getting better. I still miss you though."

I couldn't have her sit on this dresser forever. She needed to be at peace. It was time she was buried.

St. Anthony's Church was about ten minutes away. I drove there alone in hopes of finding out information about gravemarkers. I entered the rectory and Deacon Larry was sitting behind his desk.

"Excuse me. Hi, how are you?" I said.

"Hello, fine thank you. How can I help you?" the deacon said.

"Well, my name is Janet Stickmon," I began, attempting to sound professional, "and I'd like to know how to go about buying a gravemarker."

The deacon looked concerned and invited me to sit down. "Why do you need a gravemarker?"

And I played my mental tape, "Well, my mother died last year and my father, he's in a nursing home."

His eyes tightened and a wrinkle came across his brow. "Can you tell me a little bit about yourself and how your mother died?"

"Mom died last summer of liver cirrhosis and bleeding ulcers. Once my father was placed in a nursing home, I moved up here to live with my aunt and uncle on my mother's side." As I continued, his attention seemed to be compromised by something he was writing down. I ignored it and continued talking, "Right now I go to Rosemead High School and…"

By the time I finished, he looked up, his eyes softened, "Wow, you have been so matter of fact. You are quite a strong young lady." Then he leaned over his desk to hand me something. It was a check—a check which seemed to be more than enough to cover the cost of a gravestone.

My mouth hung open, still wondering if it was for me. I didn't expect him to write me a check and was embarrassed since I didn't come to the church looking for money.

"This is for you. You take this and buy a gravemarker for your mother. There's a place that sells gravestones up the street on San Gabriel Blvd. Near the florist. You can't miss it."

"Thank you, thank you so much," I said, smiling with tears in my eyes. I was so surprised by the generous gift. I thanked him again on the way out the door and immediately left to buy my mother's gravemarker. I looked forward to the day Mom would finally have a proper burial.

╬

I arrived late to Resurrection Cemetery. I was supposed to meet Fr. Mark at Mom's gravesite at 11:00 a.m., but I missed him; only an open hole in the ground was waiting for Mom and I. Disappointed and angry with myself, I just sat there, holding Momma on my lap.

Then I saw him. Fr. Mark was walking across the lawn toward me, his weightless gait making him look as if he was floating. His glasses and well-groomed beard didn't hide the peaceful countenance in his slender face.

The rolling green hills stretched for acres, punctuated by bouquets of flowers and mourning visitors. Fr. Mark stood across from me as he performed a simple burial rite for Mom. The sun was bright against our faces as we squinted. It was just he and I who laid my mother to rest.

Fr. Mark left me alone with Mom. I prayed, sitting there looking at the urn in the burial plot. I didn't cry. I just prayed, trying to recall her voice and her face.

We kept each other company in this spot. This was where I came to sing to her, where I told her all the funny things that happened at school, where I thanked her for instilling confidence in me, where I asked her for advice about boys, and where I told her about all the people I met. Mom was present there. And if I couldn't look at her face when I spoke to her, then at least I could be with her on the piece of earth that she carried.

11

The career center brought me much comfort my junior year; it reminded me that college was still in my future. I visited almost everyday, getting to know Ms. Weidemann, the career guidance counselor, quite well. When I walked in at lunch, she always told me about the latest scholarship. "It's best you start researching colleges and scholarships now so you'll be prepared for your senior year," she said with urgency and excitement in her voice.

When my senior year arrived, Ms. Weidemann guided me as if preparing to send off her own child to college. She made it her personal mission to make sure I not only made it to college but could also afford it. "You're an A student. You're active. You don't have parents. You'll have money for school," she said with conviction.

Upon her recommendation, I started with the statement of purpose a couple months early. She read, corrected, and reread it. She then made sure I correctly filled out every portion of my financial aid packet and threw every scholarship and internship opportunity in my direction: The Elk's Club, Soroptomist's Club, Bank of America Award, Inroads Internship Program, summer job fairs.

I had only one foot in the career center door when she handed me the scholarship form for the Elk's Club. She said, "Oh Janet! Good! Okay, Janet, hurry and fill this out. The deadline is in a couple of days. Sit down right here. You can use this typewriter. You don't have much time." And I sat down and began typing.

That's how everything worked that year; taking my time was never an option. And once I completed and sent off college applications to four different universities and at least ten local and national scholarships, waiting was the only thing left to do.

But I wished waiting wasn't so exhausting. I still had to graduate and for an overachiever and a perfectionist, this didn't just mean getting by. It meant maintaining my 4.22 GPA, keeping up in AP Calculus, AP English, and Physics, and remaining committed as the drum major of the band, member of a service club and the speaker's bureau, and the captain of the girl's track team. By the time the second semester came, I was completely burnt out. While other senioritis-afflicted seniors went on glamorous adventures, ditching whole days of school, the most my good girl conscience allowed me to do was ditch 6th period to mail my last college application to USC before the post office closed.

I was ready to move on and get the hell out of high school. I wasn't terribly attached to my new family. My classmates bored me and all my friends had graduated the year before. Meanwhile, the smog of the San Gabriel Valley bore holes in my lungs. I couldn't wait to go to college and live a new life.

When April 1991 came, my senioritis was full blown and people noticed. My calculus teacher wondered why I had nearly failed my last couple tests and my coaches noticed my long jump performance wasn't improving. At league trials, my sprint coach knelt next to me while I was stretching, and asked, "You're burnt out, aren't you?"

"Yeah, I guess so," I said, not realizing how obvious it was.

Tired and sweaty, I drove home from the meet, my body and will worn out. I had the whole house to myself. I took a long, quiet bath and sat in the tub for at least a half hour, scrubbing every inch of my body. I massaged lotion up and down my legs, around my feet, and between my toes as if squeezing the tension from my body. It felt good to slow down and pay attention to my body. "I can't wait until the school year is over," I thought, curling up on the couch in my pajamas.

12

When I received my acceptance letter from U.C. Irvine, I was ecstatic! It was my first choice. My school mother, Ms. Weidemann, deserved all the credit. All the last minute running around paid off since I'd been awarded enough scholarships to cover my first two years of college.

I took every chance to escape the drudgery of high school life that drug my intellect and my body. Before the school year ended, I made at least four trips to Irvine, sometimes for business, but mostly to fantasize.

I dressed up the way I envisioned a college student would dress: khaki shorts, a light pink button down shirt with a light sweater wrapped around my shoulders. I wore my hair down and put just a little bit of make-up on. With as much excitement as the day I opened my acceptance letter, I jumped in my car and drove to Irvine.

My private reverie. Wind blowing in my hair. Dreams filling my head. No one could have awakened me. The beauty of every mile along the way was magnified by my dream state. A 50-minute drive brought my clunky '78 Ford Fairmount to Irvine to be in the presence of BMW's, Lexus', and Mercedes'. As I approached the north end of campus, I saw a sign for a botanical garden ahead. It was sheltered by tall, brownish-green, grass that leaned away from Campus Road preventing you from seeing what was inside. I stuck my head out the window to breathe in the air. "Hmmm-aahhh. What a big difference!" I thought. It was a surprise to breathe in fresh air that smelled of pine instead of smog. After fumbling around trying to figure out how to get a parking permit out of the nearest machine, I finally found a place to park and stepped onto the campus for the first time.

I didn't know what dormitory I would be in, so I just walked around and explored the campus. I ended up at the center of the university where Aldrich Park was. Trees of every species enveloped the open lawn. Several paths snaked their way through the thick, lush grass allowing students to travel from one end of campus to the other. My eyes slowly followed the older students walking around, imagining myself soon walking the campus as an official student. Beside me were thick vines of honeysuckle, white and yellow blossoms releasing a fragrance reminding of my childhood and the vines that Momma grew in front of our old house that burned down. It was accompanied by a faint smell of jasmine that I couldn't locate, but definitely recognized. Strip malls, concrete, and traffic didn't clutter the area. I was surrounded by nature and didn't miss the San Gabriel Valley at all.

I moved myself in. No one helped me, but I wasn't too bothered by it. I packed my faded red Ford with all my belongings and drove back to Irvine. It was moving day for everybody. There were carts all around Middle Earth. I grabbed one, brought it to my car, loaded it, and pulled it to my room in Rivendell where I met my roommate, Jackie. When I noticed her parents helping her move in, a certain sadness came over me as I watched everyone else moving into their dorm rooms with the help of their parents and siblings. People exchanged kisses and hugs. Parents held their child's hands close to their bosoms and stared into their faces giving them some last minute advice before they left. There was much I envied that day. I couldn't do anything about it, though. I sat in my room imagining my parents sending me off to college, leaving me with a little wisdom, too. And I imagined them missing me.

Years before, my parents had left me their wisdom. Though my Mom was no longer alive and my father was still in the nursing home, they left me with enough skill, spirit, and will during my childhood that would help me get through life as a young adult. Attending a university became far more than just the escape I was looking for. It became the fulfillment of their expectations—what they hoped for, and what they once hoped for themselves. I was living out what they couldn't in their own lifetime. So, it was important that I followed through, graduating from college, not just to please them, but to please myself—to show them that they did not live in vain. I had already exceeded the expectations of all who knew my history, and there was no reason I couldn't excel during college and after graduation. Attending college became a path that transcended this life and reached out to my mother.

It seemed natural for everyone to make friends during the first couple of weeks of college; this was good for me since I rarely took much initiative to make friends. By the time the school year was underway, I found a clique of my own: Jackie, Shayra, Gina, Amy, Mitch, and Daniel. There were a few other people that came in and out of our little circle, but this was the core crew. We did everything together—ate meals in the dining hall together, studied together, celebrated birthdays together. And I cannot forget the pranks we pulled on each other—duct taping Mitch and Daniel's door shut, laying out Dixie cups filled with water in front of their door, removing one of the small hoses from the toilet to let it point in the direction of whoever was using it; when a person flushed, water shot out, making it look as though the person peed in their pants.

However, the award-winning prank happened on Gina's birthday.

The big day was a week away. Amy, Shayra, and I decided to make a fake cake made out of poster board and sponges. We cut a long strip of poster board and stapled the ends to form a circle. We then cut out a circle for the top of the cake. The sponges were placed on top and the edges were rounded out. We stuck candles into the sponges and smothered vanilla frosting with bits of chocolate chips all over our creation. We couldn't wait to see the look on Gina's face.

On her birthday, she walked into our suite, where we waited to surprise her. As we sang happy birthday, she stood behind the cake, not suspecting a thing. Gina blew out the candles, and then noticed that the center was caved in. She took the knife and stabbed the cake in the center. "Ha!" she said, as she uncovered our ploy, while the rest of us burst into a mix of laughter and disappointment.

The guys had their fun, as well. I heard them whispering and giggling about fire and farts in their room while I was standing in the bathroom. Within seconds, Daniel threw open the door, screaming. He shot through the suite and down the hallway. Meanwhile, Mitch was laughing uncontrollably. "What happened?" I asked, slightly afraid to find out.

Between laughs, he found the breath to tell me, "His fart caught on fire...Daniel bent over. I held a lighter near his butt and he farted. The flame was hhhhuge!" A week later in chemistry, all of us learned exactly why this chemical reaction happened, and we recounted the "experiment" and joked about how funny it would be if Daniel had to go to the hospital and explain to a doctor what happened.

I was never lonely with my friends. The laughs eased the pain. I didn't completely forget who and what I didn't have, but when I was with them, I did. Around my friends, I had a home. They weren't blood, but they were family.

It was open season for freshman during the first quarter. Sororities, fraternities, ethnic clubs, Christian organizations—every group leader was out recruiting. I had my own biases against sororities and had no interest in being in the company of little, rich girls with inflated levels of self-importance who lived the illusion that they were somehow popular while they purported to be a part of a service organization. I wasn't too interested in buying my friends, so I didn't bother to rush any sorority. The thought of joining the Black Student Union or *Kababayan* (the Filipino student organization) entered my mind, but at the time I believed ethnic clubs were divisive and undermined integration.

Since the wounds from senioritis were still healing, I decided not to join any clubs during the first couple quarters. I didn't know how heavy my workload would be, so I thought it best to focus on my studies. As a mathematics major (later changing to civil engineering), my workload required my complete attention. Thanks to the long hours of studying, I received A's and a couple B's during my first two quarters.

I could smell the faint jasmine again. A light breeze brushed my shoulders as I walked toward the student center along the outer circle. Two girls approached me with bright smiles, "Hi! I'm Susan and this is Brandy. We belong to a nondenominational Christian group. Would you like to come to our Easter Vigil celebration?"

I was a little curious and figured there would be no harm in going. "Sure," I said.

"Great! You'll love it. Can we take down your name and number? We'll give you a call," Susan said.

When they arrived at Middle Earth to pick me up, there were two others in the car who were also new to the group. We drove to a fancy hotel and walked into a large banquet hall. Beneath the large crystal chandelier, hundreds of people greeted one another with smiling faces before taking their seats as close as possible to the stage.

A man came to the microphone, greeting the crowd, "How's everyone tonight?" as his energy radiated from the stage. The entire presentation then became an overstimulated blur. He paced back and forth, raising his arms, lowering his arms, talking about discipleship. "We need to draw in as many disciples into our church as possible," he kept repeating, as cheers and random noise from a snare drum resounded in agreement.

When the presentation ended, people were smiling and embracing. Susan and Brandy introduced us to their friends, and they smiled and embraced us, too. Their warmth and friendliness was curious; I noticed a feigned sincerity but dismissed it, since I enjoyed watching everyone being so friendly.

On the way home, the two girls asked, "Would you be interested in doing weekly Bible studies with us?"

"Sure, okay," I said, not really knowing what the Bible studies would entail.

Later that week, I met Brandy in Aldrich Park. We read Matthew 10: 37-39, which said that whoever loves their father more than Jesus is unworthy of Him and that whoever does not "take up his cross" and follow Him is unworthy of Him. Brandy then asked me, "What religion are you?"

"I'm Catholic," I said.

Then she began to share her story of conversion, "I was raised Buddhist by my parents. But I decided to break away from that tradition because I didn't believe I was following God. Now I feel like a true disciple. What do you think it means to be a true disciple?"

"I don't know. Someone who follows God."

"Do you think you are a true Christian as a Catholic?"

I had never thought about that before. I began to doubt if I was a real Christian, "Well, I don't know. I think I am." My uncertainty gave her permission to attempt to convert me into one her church's disciples.

After spending between four and six weeks meeting with the two girls, I was beyond paranoia. I couldn't watch a half-hour of television without feeling guilty for not praying. I woke up at 6:30 a.m., opening the Bible and reading passages frantically, fearing the salvation of my soul was in jeopardy. I knew this didn't feel right, but I thought the feeling was just part of my conversion. My roommate, Jackie, noticed something was wrong. "Janet, is everything alright? You've been acting strange lately. I'm a little worried."

"Mm, no. It's these two girls," I said, telling her the entire story.

I sat at my desk and wept while considering the possibility of leaving Catholicism, a religion that my mother raised me to practice. The only lifeline of faith that linked me to my mother was Catholicism. Memories of catechism classes, communion, confirmation; the late nights Momma spent in the back seat of her car with her blanket and thermos, waiting for me to get out of my catechism class; me sharing with Momma the cookies, the cupcakes, and the lessons the catechism teacher gave our class; the priests and youth ministers who had been an inspiration to me; the apple fritter Momma bought me the day I was confirmed; the days I prayed with her in the hospital; the evenings I spent praying to God to help me survive after Mom's death; Deacon Larry paying for Mom's gravemarker; Fr. Mark burying her; the guidance and answered prayers I received from God through the people sent to help me. I did have a relationship with God—as a Catholic. To let go of the faith my mother raised me to believe in was like letting go of her. I finally decided to speak to a Catholic priest on campus.

⚗

I walked up a ramp into a small trailer called "Interfaith." The room smelled of candles; the walls were wooden panels with posted pictures of Jesus and Mary and menorahs and framed quotations. Scanning the room I noticed the words Hillel, Cantebury, and Ba'hai. I learned that Catholics not only worshipped here, but Episcopalians, Muslims, Jews, and people of many other faiths worshipped here, as well. I found the office of the Catholic chaplain, Fr. Dan Tiller, and poked my head in, "Hi, Fr. Dan? My name is Janet Stickmon. Can I talk to you for a minute?" not knowing exactly what to say next.

"Sure, sure," he said with a bright smile, "Have a seat. How can I help you?"

Getting right to the point, I asked, "What does it mean in the Catholic Church to be a disciple?"

He squinted with suspicion, his white skin turning rose against his pearly gray hair. He seemed to know where this conversation was going. He asked, "Where is this question coming from?"

"Well, during Easter, I was approached by two girls from some fellowship who have been trying to convert me."

Once I gave him the name of the group, he answered my question, "Discipleship is following God. It's not about forcing someone to do it. It is following God of your own free will, through your words and your actions. What does discipleship mean to you?"

"Well, I know it means to follow God. I guess it means being good to other people and being giving," I stuttered.

"Well, yes. See you already have an understanding of what discipleship is—as a Catholic. You see this group is an extension of a cult started in Boston. Like any cult," he continued, handing me a pamphlet on cults, "they brainwash people. What this one is known for is its emphasis on discipleship and building up their numbers."

"I was really close to converting. I didn't know what to do, so I came here."

"Well, I'm glad you did. I think you might be interested in our Newman Fellowship meetings. You're welcome to try it out. It's a group of Catholic students who get together every Wednesday. It's led by a young lady named Lisa Directo."

"Okay, maybe I'll come to the next meeting. Thank you so much Father Dan. I appreciate it."

⚟

Jackie answered the phone when Brandy called. She was about to tell her I wasn't home, when I asked her to give me the phone.

"Hello, Brandy. Well, I just want to let you know that I won't be going to your Bible studies anymore. You see, I met with a Catholic priest and he helped me sort some things out."

"Nooo! You can't! No! He's just telling you what your itching ears want to hear!!"

"Look, don't call me anymore. I'm not interested. Don't call me ever again!" I yelled, slamming down the phone.

⚟

I arrived at the trailer and discovered the meeting was in Aldrich Park. The graceful curves of one pathway led past the trees and near the center of the park, where I saw about fifteen people lying down in the grass. With a gentle voice, Lisa said, "Please get into a comfortable position and meditate for about thirty minutes." Everyone's eyes were closed, so I snuck in the middle and lied down, too. I wasn't quite sure how to meditate, so I just did what came naturally, closing my eyes, listening to my surroundings. I felt a light breeze blow across my face. Ravens were calling out to each other. I opened my eyes to see one fly overhead and into the trees. An orange haze bled across the soft blue sky as the sun set. I stared at clouds watching them take the shape of animals, wondering why I never noticed them before, thinking how rare it was that I ever sat still and relaxed; these things in nature exist whether I noticed or not. The thirty minutes were over. People stretched and sighed, thanking Lisa for the time to meditate.

"Now, you'll need a partner for this next exercise," Lisa said, "Once you find a partner, one person must close their eyes while the other leads their partner back to Interfaith. This is called a trust walk."

I found a partner and ended up being the one to close my eyes. My cautious baby steps led me to believe I wouldn't trip or bump into something. It was awkward being led back by a stranger. I was agitated, having grown used to being independent and in control; but, it was also calming to know that someone I could trust would lead me where I needed to be. When everyone arrived at the trailer, we shared our experiences.

Lisa then explained, "Yes, this models our relationship with God. We are not always in control and must rely on His help and sometimes the help of others." With that in mind, I decided to come to the following meeting. This time, I felt like I was in the right place.

⟊

I was still a young woman used to surviving, trusting few people. My shell was callous enough to protect me but permeable enough to allow the good in. I acquired a hypersensitive emotional radar, able to detect the authenticity of a person's character nearly without flaw. I doubt this heightened sense would have developed had I not lost so much. Few made it through.

⟊

Gary, a man I met at my first Newman Fellowship meeting, approached me while I was outside the Physical Science Lecture Hall, waiting for Calculus class to begin. "How are you?" he asked.

"Mmm. Not so good. I'm really stressed out," I replied, feeling exhausted beyond relief.

We spoke for a short while before he began to tell me a story, "There was a little boy who saw all these starfish washed ashore. He started tossing them back into the ocean one by one. An older man came out of nowhere, yelling, 'Why are you throwing all of them back in? There are too many. Ah! You're just wasting your time! That won't make any difference!' The boy then picks up another starfish and says, 'Well, it makes a difference to this one,' as he throws it back into the water."

I was that starfish, and for every story Gary told, I always saw myself as the central character being freed and empowered. Gary was not just a chemistry researcher and professor, but he was also a man invested in the struggle for liberation—spiritual, emotional, and physical. He drew my attention to the oppression experienced by women, people of color, and the poor, recommending books to me like *Markings*, *I Know Why the Caged Bird Sings*, *The Night is Dark and I'm Far From Home*, and *Pedagogy of the Oppressed*.

Gary represented stability to me, as he did to several others. He seemed to have a following, people who sought his consolation at every hour of the day: people who were depressed, women mistreated by their boyfriends, sex addicts who just needed someone to talk to. To me, he was a gentle, compassionate man who I could always turn to when life seemed hopeless. He was the anchor that reminded me that no matter what happens in our lives, we never become less than human. He'd say, "People just want to know that they are 'okay.' I don't think when people say that they want to be happy in life that that is what they really mean. I think people want to be content. I think that is what people really want."

Pondering my own dream to "just be happy," I began to wonder if it was happiness that I was truly looking for. Did I want to smile everyday and be filled with utter joy from morning 'til night? Or did I want to be at peace with myself—satisfied with my life and the person I had become? I juggled this idea along with Gary's other daily lessons toted in my head, like, "Be kind to yourself," and "Take time to speak to the daisies," and "There are no right or wrong decisions. One grows regardless of what path one takes." I reveled in these new insights, growing more pensive, freeing myself of old thoughts that confined me.

⚏

I was inundated with things to do at Interfaith, but I didn't mind. Every act seemed to not only rejuvenate my faith, but reveal new gifts I never knew I had; I was discovering my gifts faster than I could keep up with them: singing with the music ministry, planning retreats and weekly meetings, sharing insights about faith and purpose with friends and strangers, learning the art of small talk to weave myself in out of conversations.

And when I shared my history, people at Interfaith, like Gary, were compassionate and accepting, never judgmental or filled with pity. They accepted me for everything that I was, including my broken past. Because of their unconditional acceptance, I trusted them, finding that confidentiality was what I needed to feel safe enough to trust. And as others shared their stories of brokenness with me, I learned to keep their words confidential, as well, recognizing the sacredness of what was shared from the heart.

Lisa was another person I trusted. The more meetings I went to, the more I learned how beautiful she was: pensive and intuitive, sincere and gentle. Lisa was a healer, having the undeniable gift to console people with the right words and a warm hug. She understood my thoughts when I was still trying to make sense of them, never pretending to have all the answers; by sharing her own struggles with life and her faith, she gave me a glimpse of what it meant to question God and still be prayerful—that our relationships with God were meant to be dialogues.

I came to her, high on faith, excited about the many places in life I was noticing God's presence. With a calm response, she said, "Yes, I think these situations regularly and readily exist in our lives. It's not that all of a sudden these new life-giving events are entering your life; they have always been present. It's just that now you are seeing them in a new light...a light that displays God's presence in everyday situations and in the people who regularly, and not so regularly, surround us."

13

I was back with Auntie Pacita and Tatay for the summer and stayed in a room, about 8' wide and 10' long, with a partition separating it from the back of the kitchen. The baby blue room felt more like a childhood fort than a bedroom. Looking in the mirror, I put on my blue and gold-checkered top and gold slacks, trying to look my best for a morning interview with a modeling agency in Beverly Hills. Loud pounding came through my bedroom door, "Janet, I want to talk to you!" I knew the woman's voice. My heart pressed against my chest, as I opened the door and walked into the livingroom.

Rovalia sat on the couch, waiting for me. She was my aunt and uncle's oldest daughter, the oldest of twelve children. In her forties, with three children, Rovalia's domineering character won her no allies, especially amongst her siblings. Her manipulative nature pulsed shallow beneath her skin and escaped from her mouth, writhing with every malicious word she spoke. She was the one who once walked into the house, uninvited, passed by my room when it was messy, and asked my aunt and uncle, "Why is she here? Why are you taking her back? Look. Her room is dirty. Yeah, that's how Black people are."

I sat down on the couch next to her, holding a pillow in my lap. Tatay was in the kitchen and Auntie Pacita was sitting near the window. I sat confident, ashamed of nothing, remembering Auntie warning me that she'd come.

"Oh, you're all dressed up," Rovalia said, looking at me, head to toe.

"I have an interview," I said coldly.

"Well. I just wanted to tell you that since you are not contributing money for rent or for groceries, next summer you have to find another place to live. You are 18 now. You are an adult. It's time you stopped taking a freebee from my parents. I give freely. I don't give with strings attached. My sister, Alma, is planning to come here from the Philippines and she will have to stay here. You are just, what, a second degree cousin to my father! Charity starts first with the family!"

A rush of hot tears filled my eyes, but weren't permitted to fall, not in her presence. Auntie Pacita sat, without a word in my defense, looking out the window. Tatay sat near the other window, also in silence. Did they want this to happen? Wondering how the situation reached this point, I remembered Auntie Pacita telling me, "Rovalia will come to talk to you about paying rent. Just tell her dat you are and dat you will continue, ha. You don't hab to gib me anything because I know you are going to school. You hab to sabe por school. Sabe dat money, ha. Because I cannot support you during the school year. I like you, you don't hab to pay me because I like you…" I offered money for groceries, but she refused it. I planned to give her some money from my next check anyway.

Auntie knew all of this. Why didn't she say something? Did Auntie and Tatay really want me out of the house? Since they said nothing, I assumed they did.

"Well, I have to leave for my interview," I said, hiding my fear and confusion.

"As long as you're living with my parents for the next month and a half, you have to give my parents money for groceries."

"Okay," I said, not wanting to argue, leaving out the back door.

Sucking my tears in, I got into my car and drove to Beverly Hills. With a composure that masked my morning confrontation, I walked into my interview. "Hello, I'm Ms. Pearcy. Please have a seat," she said, "Now what are you interested in?"

"I'm interested in maybe doing commercials or maybe some modeling for store advertisements." I didn't tell her that some of my friends encouraged me to try modeling; I thought it would be a good chance to earn extra money for college.

"Well, you have the look, but you need some professional photographs. A decent set will cost you at least $200. And you'll need an agent. You have to be ready…listening and waiting for messages from your agent. You need to be willing to eat, drink, and sleep the entertainment industry."

I swallowed, knowing my hopes for breaking into modeling didn't run that deep. "College is my first priority," I said.

"Well, education will have to come second," she replied without remorse. That statement alone helped me make my decision. I wasn't willing to sacrifice my education for a slim chance of appearing in a commercial or some television show.

Disappointed, I began my drive home, and once I hit the 10 Freeway, I finally allowed myself to cry—not about the interview, but about being kicked out. With questions spinning through my mind, I wept and shook uncontrollably: Who was telling her I wasn't paying rent? Are my aunt and uncle trying to get me out of their house? Were they afraid to tell me themselves? Where am I going to live next summer? Am I going to be out on the streets?

And, what was this about a freebee? Was that bitch calling the love Auntie and Tatay gave me, a freebee? Love could never be called a freebee. I never took for granted anything they gave to me. I always told them and showed them how grateful I was. *I* was the one who offered to help with household expenses and Auntie declined!

When I arrived home, Auntie and Tatay were in their bedroom. I walked in and asked, "So, is it true? Do you want me to leave?"

"No, you can stay here as long as you want," Tatay said, "Until you hab a husband, you can stay here," trying to get me to crack a smile.

"No, Jinit, you can stay. It's okay," Auntie added. This confused me. They didn't defend me at the time and then they're telling me this!

"Why didn't you say something then?" I asked.

"I don't want to make it bigger," Auntie said, "You know Rovalia's mouth. So, I just estay quiet. I don't want to make it bigger." I wasn't convinced. Feeling like a yoyo, I tried deciding who to believe. They didn't want to aggravate the situation, so they didn't say anything? If they really wanted me there, they would have defended me, I thought.

⌗

Within a couple days, I gave $50 to Auntie and Tatay for groceries. It wasn't much, but it was something. The day after, the phone rang. Remi answered it and handed it to me.

"Janet, I heard that you gave money to my parents, but you only contributed $50. That's not enough!" Rovalia's tirade began.

"That's all I had! You know money doesn't grow on trees!" I shouted, wishing I could have come up with a better come back than that. I hung up the phone, crying. I ran into one of the bedrooms, locking the door.

"God why is this happening to me," I prayed, kneeling over a clothes hamper in the dark. "If Mom didn't die, none of this would have ever happened. What am I going to do? Who told her how much I gave to Auntie? Someone is leaking out information to Rovalia."

I came out of the room with dry tear marks on my face, and knelt at Auntie's feet. She held and comforted me, "It's okay, Jinit don't cry. But Jinit, please apologize to Rovalia. Apologize for me."

"Okay, I'll apologize for you."

I called Rovalia back. "Sorry. Sorry for being disrespectful," I said, knowing that bitch didn't deserve it. I only apologized so Auntie would be at peace. I regretted it, deeply regretted it. If anything, *I* deserved the apology. She was the first to make me feel like a nobody. She could have been more tactful, gentler. But, she wasn't. She chose to use her nasty machine-gun-like mouth to plant fear into me—the only way her small mind knew how.

One question still remained: Who was reporting my every action to Rovalia? Who told her how much I gave to Auntie? Was it my aunt or uncle? It couldn't have been them, unless Rovalia forced them to tell. Or was it my cousin, Remi? No, I thought she was beginning to like me. I used to listen to her problems and give her advice. She'd always thank me and mid-sentence, say, "Oh. Jinit. I like your color. Look at me I'm so pale."

But, she also had an evil streak. It wasn't beneath her to be rude and ignorant, mocking me because I always studied, never wanting me to do homework on the kitchen table, seeing my dishes in the sink and mumbling, "That Black...don't know how to wash dishes!" not knowing other people in the house could hear her. Yes, I bet it was Remi.

‡

A month later, I was waiting for the bus on the corner of Francisquito and Sunset Avenue, thinking about how different Mom was from Auntie Pacita, how Mom would have defended me. I wasn't eager to return home. I was so tired, I nearly dosed off sitting in the grass with my head between my knees and my ankles crossed. When, I opened my eyes, walking down the sidewalk was an African-American man in his twenties wearing a white trench coat, a Tijuana straw hat with a pink feather stuck in the side, and two earrings dangling from one ear. He sat down beside me and said, "Hey! How can you sleep in this weather?"

I smiled.

"Well, I'm not waiting for the bus, myself. I was just walking around so I could sit next to a pretty girl like you," the man continued.

I smiled.

He then looked at me and said, "Hmm. You're an interesting mix! What are you?"

Although people had always been curious about what I was mixed with, no one had ever phrased it quite like that before. "I'm half Black and half Filipino," I said.

"Which side is Black and which side is Filipino?"

"My mother is Filipino. From Cebu. And my father is Black. From Shreveport, Louisiana."

"I once dated a girl who was Filipino. Her family was so disappointed. They didn't like at all that she was dating a Black man. Did the Filipino side of your family have trouble with your father being Black? Did they accept him?"

"I'm not sure. I don't think they minded. I don't know." To be honest, the thought never entered my mind. The question was disturbing. I didn't want to believe that the Filipino side of my family had trouble with my father being Black.

"Well, you better find out," he said, "Chances are your parents probably have a different story. I know I had a lot of trouble with my girlfriend's family. We ended up breaking up."

My bus pulled up to the curb. I was interested in talking some more and yet I was also eager to get on the bus. "Well, my bus is here. I have to go. It was good talking to you," I said politely.

"Remember what I told you. Go find out if your family really accepted your father."

14

For over a month, I woke up every morning, trembling, nerves taut, feeling someone spying on me, reporting all my actions to Rovalia. I tried to stay out of the house as long as possible. If I wasn't at work, I was with Anabelle. If I wasn't with Anabelle, then I was at Tai Chi class. But no matter where I was, Rovalia's presence haunted me, festering within.

I counted down the days until school started, looking forward to being free again. I wanted so badly to be on my own, experiencing life on my own terms. "Why be in a house where you're unwanted, when you could be alone?" I'd lie in bed thinking at night, trembling more fiercely than in the daytime.

⊥⊤

A poster of "Life's Little Instructions" hung on the wall near the hallway. A beautiful shoreline with palm trees and turquoise skies was embroidered in a rug that hung over our couch in the livingroom. Shayra added the finishing touch to our new apartment: a braided woolen drape interwoven with wooden beads that dangled in the doorway to the hall.

When I moved in with Gina, Amy, and Shayra, I was relieved to be back in Irvine. It was a new place for us to be family, still celebrating birthdays and studying, but this time having even more fun testing out our families' recipes on each other and pretending to be Wanda from *In Living Color*.

By this time, Da'y was transferred from the nursing home in Lancaster to one in the Bay Area. Lou, Dana, and Jill wanted to have him close by so he would get more visitors. As usual, I was busy with school and trying to figure out what would become of me the following summer. An opportunity to do research with a professor on campus through the McNair STAR Program came up, and I finally received an application. With the spare time I had between classes, I began working on it, hoping that somehow it might lead to a summer opportunity to do research.

On Thursday, November 12, 1992, I had a dream that I was in Lancaster, waiting on 10th Street East, next to the fence where Mom used to pick me up after school. My best friend from high school, Deanna, was running down the street toward me, saying, "Your mom told me that you need to pack up all your dad's things. Put all his clothes and belongings in his suitcase because she is going to pick him up. She was very angry and impatient." For the next couple of days, I tried interpreting the dream. Why was Mom mad? Does she want me to visit him more often? Did I end up forgetting about him, getting too caught up with school? Sick of thinking about it, I continued working on my application, not telling anyone about the dream.

At about 7:00 a.m. on Saturday, November 14, 1992, I received a call from Lou, "Janet. I'm sorry. Fermon expired."

"Expired? What do you mean? He died? Daddy died?!"

"Yes," he replied.

My brother had a ticket waiting for me on will call. When I arrived, we still needed to choose a casket for Da'y and purchase a burial plot. We looked around the funeral parlor noticing how expensive the caskets were. A decent one cost $2500 while the cheapest one, a plywood box, cost about $200. "God, dying is expensive," I thought.

We were asked to view Daddy's body. I was by myself when I peaked in. The room was cold, with curtains draped everywhere. Da'y looked different. Skinnier than I remember. His nose flatter and slightly crooked. Da'y lived to the age of 80. Since his life didn't seem cut short, I wasn't as upset at his passing as I was when Momma passed. But, I still missed him. After spending a few moments there, my mind became blank. I left feeling numb, and walked around the chapel adjacent to the funeral parlor. Dazed, I took one step at a time. Slowly. My mind still empty. I looked at the stained glass and noticed the deep blues and reds cast upon the pews, the wooden columns separating the narrow walkway from the chapel, the vapid smelling air.

Lou, Dana, and I drove to Rolling Hills Cemetery, comparing the prices of burial plots and niches, agreeing to buy a niche for our father. The gentleman who helped us punched lists of numbers into his calculator, saying, "Let's see here," as he coughed and wheezed between calculations. With each breath, his nose whistled. Lou leaned toward me and said, "Ooo! He sound like he 'bout to go, too!" Thinking the same thing, I covered my mouth, trying hard not to laugh.

╬

Da'y wore a three-piece suit that Lou, Dana, and Jill bought for him. It was the first suit I'd ever seen him wear. He looked sharp. The way he did in his younger years. And he lied in the casket with a peaceful expression, as if smiling.

All at the funeral wore black. Black sweaters, black dresses, black slacks, black hats. I sat next to Mama Lila and Jill. Lou and Dana were behind us. The funeral service began and Lodie Mae, also known as Punkin, gave her final respects. Punkin had her reading glasses on but could barely read a page from Scripture. She kept adjusting her glasses, moving closer and closer to the page until her face was two inches from the Bible. Lou and Dana giggled. I turned around, staring at them as if warning children to be quiet in church, not wanting to admit that I thought it was funny, too.

Mama Lila took the podium. "Fermon was a good man and a very hardworker," she said with conviction. Her eloquence and grace when describing the man in whom she once believed the "sun rose and set" was beautiful. I sat amazed and impressed by her respect and praise for a man who hadn't always treated her with the same honor. Then she looked at me, "And as for Janet, his youngest daughter, suffering the loss of her father after having already lost her mother, I want you to know that you will always have another mother to turn to."

It was the most selfless gesture I'd ever witnessed. How was it possible for a woman to love the child from her ex-husband's second marriage? I wasn't sure.

╬

As I walked to my Calculus 2D class, my feelings were raw. Da'y's death made it official that I was an orphan. More alone than ever. When I saw my friend, Cara, near the door, she said nothing and just opened her arms to hug me. I began to weep, surprising myself since I cried little during the funeral.

I was afraid to step into the classroom. I sat near the back so no one I recognized could see me, just in case I'd start crying again. I sat down slowly, took out my notebook and tried to focus. I took notes, not concentrating, but wondering still what would become of me.

15

In 1993, I was accepted into the McNair Star Program to do research in chaotic dynamical systems with Professor Edriss Titi. The coordinator, Sara Gavin, organized the program, ensuring that students from underrepresented racial backgrounds were trained to do research and prepared to pursue advanced degrees.

The group was predominantly African-American and Latino-American, with one white student who was part Native-American. Aside from family, it was my first time being in a group of people of color. I was very uncomfortable; I didn't understand why it was important to have a program that served only people of minority backgrounds. At an orientation meeting, Sara explained, "There are very few people of color who pursue graduate degrees. Many people of minority backgrounds don't know it's possible because they are not surrounded by anyone in their family who has an advanced degree. Some don't know it's a viable option. Many don't think there's money out there for it. Well, through this program, not only will you do research with a professor on campus, but you will also be trained to research fellowships and universities best suited for your graduate career and discover how a master's or a doctorate can make you more competitive in the job market."

My discomfort didn't fade instantly, as I noticed one other student who was uncomfortable—the single white student. He spoke little to others in the group, never spending too much time socializing with us. I silently commiserated with him, imagining how awkward it must feel to be the only white person in the group.

Over the next few months, his discomfort and his distance began to speak volumes, and my sympathy wore off. He wasn't the quiet type; on campus, he was found socializing, studying, and eating lunch with his friends who were all white—the fraternity and sorority "types." Then it became obvious: he didn't identify himself as a person of color. He was benefiting from the training offered by the program by admitting to his fraction of Native-American blood while not feeling the slightest bit connected to the rest of us. I began to wonder how many other white people are still so very uncomfortable being around people of color. Perhaps, he was getting a small taste of how I felt being surrounded by upper and middle class white people everywhere I went in Irvine and Newport Beach and Costa Mesa and any other city in most of Orange County. And maybe I was getting a taste of what it would feel like if people of color were the majority everywhere we traveled.

By the time the school year was over, I became more comfortable being part of the group, discovering that I wouldn't have learned about graduate school and fellowships if not for Sara and the McNair program. I felt a new sense of pride. And at the same time, the program opened up a number of possibilities which soon filled up my next couple summers: first, the Summer Institute on High Performance Computing at the University of Minnesota Army High Performance Computing Research Center and then UCLA's summer research program the following year.

╬

When I arrived at UCLA, I drove up to Rieber Hall, not looking forward to meeting new people. I sat in my car for a few minutes before unloading my suitcases. I walked up to the registration desk and was given the key to my dorm room.

I met the others in the group at the orientation meeting. There were about 30 students from universities all over the country: Yale, Amherst, University of Hawaii, UC Berkeley. They majored in everything from biology and engineering to sociology and literature. And everyone was African-American, Latino-American, Asian Pacific Islander-American, Native-American, or a mix thereof.

Nearly all the students did research in some way related to their ethnic heritage, except for me: I was studying the origin of continental basalts in the geology department. I found myself in the company of "cultural revolutionaries"—people who knew about their cultural heritage, who were informed about racial construction, ethnic identity, and power, who had read tons of books on the history of colonization of indigenous people around the world. I was out of my league. I was only on the cusp of talking about racial issues, fearing I'd be labeled as a person who "places too much emphasis on race" or is "too angry." I knew nothing about these things. I knew about chaos theory and partial differential equations and oxidation states and exothermic reactions. Compared to the other students, I barely knew a thing about both my heritages. But, this didn't keep me from listening.

At a Chinese restaurant, Ashley explained to me the latest developments in the Hawaiian sovereignty movement and recommended I read *From A Native Daughter* by her professor, Haunani Kay Trask; she told me how her grandma used to say so proudly, "Look, that's Ashley! That's my granddaughter getting arrested!" when she saw her on TV protesting. My roommate, Sherry, stayed up late at night telling me about her research on Grier and

Cobbs' *Black Rage* and how crazy Freak-Nic in Atlanta was and what it's like being in a Black sorority.

And on the way to Mass, Irma, Edgar, and I shared the love we had for our Filipino sisters and brothers despite our common experiences of Filipino guilt and getting a whoopin' from our moms who always asked, "Do you want some more? Stop crying, ha! You want some more?" In their company, I learned from their love for the Philippines and their desire to always be connected to their homeland; through them, I decided it was crucial to one day visit Cebu, where my mother grew up.

In a room up the hall, six people piled onto two beds, taking turns talking: "I grew up in the 'hood," Leticia, from Yale, said, "And I plan on raisin' my kids in the 'hood, too, so they can have some street smarts."

"Yeah, there's no need to assimilate into mainstream white culture. We have to stop hating ourselves and where we come from. We have to be proud," said Irma.

"You know some people think that talking about race and being proud of where we come from is divisive," said another.

"Wait a minute! But culture shapes and influences the way we speak, the way we think, the way we exist. It's not divisive. It's what makes us distinct," Ashley stressed.

"That makes sense," I thought to myself, soaking in all that was said, having my entire worldview broken open. I believed that unity was achieved through learning about similarities between cultures and downplaying the differences. But what Ashley said changed everything: we can celebrate our differences and at the same time recognize our similarities! I didn't have to be the white girls I was bombarded with on TV and in magazines. I didn't have to hate myself for how I looked. I couldn't wait to return to

Irvine and share the lasting impression these conversations left on me.

16

When I returned to Irvine, it was no longer beautiful to me. It was an artificial city with finely manicured lawns and homes painted virtually the same four colors. I began hearing stories of homeless people being paid to take buses to neighboring cities, just so they wouldn't be seen. I saw white people, particularly upper/middle class white people, sheltering themselves from the world around them with their fancy cars and their planned communities. As I noticed the elitism of white students in fraternities and sororities, I felt ill. They were no longer my standard of beauty or my measure of success. An inner contempt grew within me that I'd never experienced before. And I thought about the friends I made in high school and college who were white. How would what I learned at UCLA change things? What would stay the same?

My passion for Catholicism persisted. Within a couple months, my memories of UCLA gradually took a back seat to my involvement at Interfaith. I went from being a lector, music minister, and organizer for Newman meetings and retreats to being one of the coordinators of a group called Catholic Presence. This group encouraged dialogues and collaborative efforts between Catholics and Protestants at a time when several Protestant groups on campus wanted to convert us to "true" Christianity and exclude us from a "unifying" Christian body called GO! Our group discredited misconceptions about Catholics and learned about the various Protestant beliefs through engaging in debates with the leaders of Protestant fellowships and attending their fellowship meetings.

Through Catholic Presence and the controversy with GO!, I spent every moment learning reasons behind Catholic beliefs and rituals. Mid-afternoon, I sat on the couch with a pen and pad, reading chapters from *The Faith of Our Fathers* and *Catholicism and Fundamentalism*, taking notes on the sacrifice of the Mass and infant baptism versus adult baptism. At night, between engineering assignments, I sat in a wooden cubicle highlighting lines and lines of text from pamphlets on what Catholics believe about salvation, about Mary, about the saints. As more questions surfaced, I immediately brought them to the other coordinators or to Fr. Dan, got my answers, and returned to my Bible, Bible commentary, concordance, and my stacks of Catholic literature.

Long after dark, my roommate already asleep, I stayed up late in bed, reading *Theology for Beginners* beneath the lamp. Skipping to the pages on Mary, I came upon the words "possessed of grace at every instant" and pictured a woman who, with each step, never faltered; she lilted on an invisible presence that guided her every action so that it was nothing short of loving and selfless. Curious, I flipped to the pages on grace and saw the words, "…grace simply means a free gift of God…"; but it went on to distinguish between sanctifying grace and actual grace: sanctifying grace being grace that "indwells the soul and abides in it" and actual grace being like "the wind that blows for awhile and then is gone." My heart beating fast, I continued reading, finding a line about the gifts of the Holy Spirit and how they "catch the wind of actual grace when it blows, so that we respond to it, and respond fruitfully." With Frank Sheed's book still in hand, I looked away, past the blur of books and unfinished homework, feeling a warm sensation of relief in my chest; I envisioned leaves being blown in the wind and me reaching up and catching them. I saw Mary gliding upon ribbons of grace curling in midair. And I saw myself being carried by grace and taking every chance that blew in the wind to be loving and selfless. I sensed that before birth God breathed a spirit into me that was special, a special will to live, to love. Flash frames whizzed through my head, replaying the old house burning down, Mom and Da'y dying, Rovalia kicking me out of the house, and I wondered why I still wanted to live. That must have been a gift. And then I realized God left me with much more: the gift of being disciplined and persistent, of loving to laugh and making others laugh, of listening and giving, of loving to write and draw and sing, of public speaking and being athletic; and all the strangers, friends, and relatives, as well—the people who loved me and inspired me to live, dream, and be inquisitive—people like Mom, Da'y, Lou, Mama Lila, Auntie Pacita, Tatay, Anabelle, Mr. Shepardson and his family, Ms. Weidemann, Lisa, Gary. I was a living testament of how God could transform a broken spirit; I could only believe that with what I was given, God was preparing me for something.

☩

The Newman Fellowship was turning into a different place: hyperintellectuals analyzing every word uttered, interrupting a person's feelings and reflections with unwelcomed critiques; recent converts to Catholicism damning their Protestant backgrounds to convince themselves they made the right decision; Catholics so proud of our religion's 2000 year-old heritage that they saw the beauty in nothing else. Lisa and Gary were long gone from

Interfaith, and I missed the reflective, respectful atmosphere that once attracted me to the group.

Bao, one of the coordinators of Catholic Presence, told me about another group that met at Interfaith—*Ha't C'ai*, the Vietnamese Catholic Fellowship. "*Ha't C'ai* means 'The Mustard Seeds' in Vietnamese. We're a family. We meditate, share, and eat together," Bao said proudly. Yes, they sounded close, like a family; I longed for a fellowship like that; without Bao saying so, I imagined it was a peaceful setting where noone's reflections would be critiqued or judged.

17

"Add the mint, cilantro, and the bean sprouts. Squeeze some lime juice and hoisin sauce on top. Maybe some hot sauce, if you want," Tuan, a member of *Ha't C'ai*, patiently showed me. Holding a pair of chopsticks in my right hand and a spoon in my left, I listened carefully, "Okay, you got the chopsticks? Okay, so what you want to do is get the noodles with the chopsticks and have the spoon with a little soup underneath it, like this." This was the second time I was learning how to use chopsticks, but the first time learning how to eat *pho*. I had the noodles for a second until the tangled bundle splashed back into the soup.

I tried again, "Like this?" I said, hoping I'd get it right this time.

"Yeah."

The noodles made it into my mouth, as I quickly washed them down with a spoonful of soup. Tuan and I laughed and laughed as I did it a second and then a third time until I finished the whole bowl.

Tuan, affectionately called *Ra'ch Me'p,* meaning "ripped mouth" in Vietnamese, was the most welcoming person in the whole group. Tuan immigrated to the United States as a child, traveling first by boat to a refugee camp in the Philippines and then to the U.S.

Tuan was absolutely crazy: the type of person who was witty and free with his jokes and free with his entire self. Tuan had few inhibitions, and there was no telling what he would say or do. Even though there were times I was even worried about what might come out of his mouth, I loved his spontaneity. He was one of the few people whose life was not governed by what was politically correct; consequences were of little concern to him.

Walking through Aldrich Park, near the honeysuckle vines, Tuan said, "You know, you're my first Black friend."

A little unsure how to take this, I said, "Well, as long as you know what you see on TV isn't how all Black people are. Black people have been done a great disservice by how we're portrayed on the Ricki Lake Show and every other talk show." We shared conversations like these on the phone, over email, in-person; he taught me Vietnamese words, told me stories of Vietnamese families, and showed me how to respond after a person shares during a *H'at Ca'i* meetings: rubbing his palms together lightly, making the sound of leaves rustling; I told him stories about Auntie Pacita and Tatay, about Lou and Mama Lila, and what I missed about my parents. Tuan and I talked about everything from race to faith—sharing what we loved, what we hated, and what we didn't understand. We became so close we nicknamed each other "bag of oats" and "bag of beans," coming from an episode of *The Cosby Show*, when Cliff asks Theo, "What am I? A bag of oats!!"

Others noticed our chemistry, too, as we spent more time together and took opportunities to tell everyone about the funniest things that happened to us: "Oh, you know what Tuan did?" I'd begin, already on the brink of laughter, "Oh God, let me tell you. One time at a Mustard Seed meeting, everybody was meditating, right. Tuan was laying down on his back and the oil lamp was close to his feet. I was sitting up. And for some reason, I opened my eyes. Tuan's foot was on fire! I just pointed at his foot!"

"Yeah, I felt my foot heating up and you didn't even say anything," he said to me.

"I couldn't! I didn't want to wake up everyone meditating! And then he started pounding his foot on the floor, trying to put the fire out," I said, Tuan and I both stomping our feet on the ground.

"...and flapping my arms," Tuan interrupted looking like a bird.

"He was trying so hard not to disturb the meditation. I was crackin' up. I couldn't breath!" I said with tears in my eyes, Tuan and I still laughing. Then a guy from Newman, the one known for analyzing things to death, bursts in, "Do you guys like each other?" And there I was—back again in my elementary school cafeteria hearing someone yell the same thing to Scott and I.

"No!" both of us said, feeling insulted and frustrated by the suggestion.

As we walked away, Tuan said, "You know that's the second time I've been asked that."

"I'm surprised that people's idea of intimacy is so narrow."

"Yeah, it doesn't allow for two people to have a close friendship like ours." The question never kept us from being friends. We knew our relationship better than anyone else.

⌗

At Sunday Mass, I read the first reading, ran across the room to sing the responsorial psalm with the choir, and later made an announcement for a Catholic Presence meeting taking place later that week. I'd had been doing this for nearly three years, gradually mastering the living posture of hospitality: gracious, gentle, giving, vibrant, big smile, bright eyes. But, it was draining. What was once energizing was now exhausting.

I saw Lisa in the congregation after Mass. She saw me, and we left together.

"Lisa, do you have a minute?" I asked. Tears ran down my face the moment we stepped out of the trailer. She put her arm around me as we walked down the ramp. "I'm burnt out," I told her, "I can't do this anymore."

"I can tell," she said.

As we sat in her car, Lisa said, "Sometimes we keep pedaling on a bicycle that we know is broken. That doesn't stop us. We continue pedaling, believing we're getting somewhere, but we're still in the same place." I understood. I thought I was getting somewhere, reaching a deeper faith. With every newly found ability, I was excited and somehow believed that by giving up a chance to use my gifts at Interfaith, I was giving up a chance to serve God. It never occurred to me that I would get tired.

My grades had fallen to C's and D's, and I couldn't understand why. I was studying, but doing horribly on exams. It was the beginning of my fifth year at Irvine. None of my engineering classes were making sense to me. I received a letter from the administration office that said I was on academic probation. Two more quarters on academic probation, and I would be kicked out of school.

I went to my apartment, turned on the stereo to play *Allegri Miserere*, and fell before the crucifix on the wall. Weeping and imagining I was in the Garden of Gethsamene, I pleaded, "God, what I'm I going to do? If I don't graduate, I won't get a job. God please help me. Please, please help. Please." It seemed my life's worth of tragedies were finally made manifest in my grades. I depended on my good grades as a source of confidence, keeping me from dwelling on the death of my parents. But those grades fell, and all my losses resurfaced, feeling fresher and more agonizing than ever. My spiritual needs were being met, so I thought. But, I'd been ignoring other needs—emotional, academic, physical. How was it possible that my spiritual needs we being fed, while my human needs were starved? I had always been taught that if I "put God first," then the rest of my life would fall into place. But instead, it was falling apart.

Perhaps, it was how I put God first—spending every spare moment at the Interfaith trailer praying, organizing, socializing; some of that time should have been spent studying. While in prayer, the decision was clear, but I didn't want to accept it: I'd have to leave Interfaith and spend more time studying.

Walking toward Cornerstone Café, I ran into Tuan. "Hey Bag of Beans! How are…" his pert spirit stifled by the look in my eye, "What's wrong?"

"I have to stop coming to Interfaith. It's taking too much time, and I have to get my grades up. I'm on academic probation. I might not graduate. My life is falling apart, Tuan."

He listened. His expression told me he understood I had to do whatever would help me graduate. Tuan looked down at the ground and pulled out a wooden cross from his pocket. "Here, I want you to have this. It belonged to my grandmother. I keep it with me all the time. But I want you to have it."

I clasped it in my hand, crying. We hugged as if we'd never see each other again. "Thank you, Tuan. I'm sorry, I have to go. I have to meet someone at Cornerstone. I'll see you."

"Call me, Janet, okay?"

"Okay."

I walked away wondering if instead of quitting Interfaith cold turkey, I should just limit how much time I spent there. Feeling like a junkie, I decided it would be best to sever myself completely. I was addicted to something I found in those trailer walls. And I didn't think I'd find it anywhere else.

⊥⊤

When I arrived at Cornerstone, Sara Gavin was waiting for me. I sat down across from her as we talked over coffee.

"Sara, I'm stressed…I'm really stressed out. I'm failing my classes. I decided to stop going to Interfaith. I don't even know if I'm going to graduate next year," I said, feeling embarrassed that I was sobbing so hard.

Sara leaned across the table holding my hand, looking me dead in the eye and said, "You need to go to counseling." She was serious.

God! Was I that bad? I must have been, judging from the urgency and gravity in her voice; she gave me no chance to dismiss what she was telling me. "I have a friend at the counseling office, Dr. Joe Canes. I think it would be good for you to see him."

I wasted no time. I walked to the main library and picked up a campus phone, fingers trembling as I dialed. When I asked to set an appointment with Dr. Canes, I was near tears thinking of the stigma associated with seeing a psychologist. It was tragic to me that I was in such horrible shape that I needed somebody to straighten out my wits.

I was nervous and embarrassed when I sat in the waiting room. Then Dr. Canes came down the hallway to greet me. He was a big man, with a calm and friendly face.

During that first visit, I began reciting words repeated over the past seven years whenever I made the decision to trust someone, "Well, when I was 13, my house burned down. Then when I was 15, my mom passed away. When I was 18, I was kicked out of the house. And then four months later, my dad passed away." And for the following eight weeks, every Monday, Dr. Canes asked me questions that tore through my rehearsed internal tape. Unraveling my emotions so regularly and then attempting to regain the composure to do homework exhausted me. I wasn't sure I'd make it through the next couple of months.

At the next visit, I sat cold stiff on top of my hands in Dr. Canes office, watching him as he sat across from me. He was leaning back in his reclining chair, tossing an eraser up in the air over and over again. He appeared disinterested; later, I got the impression that this was some tactic used to get me to relax and forget he was a psychologist. It worked.

"Now, why were you kicked out of the house? What happened?" he asked.

"Rovalia, my aunt and uncle's oldest daughter, knocked on my bedroom door, telling me she wanted to talk to me," I said, having no difficulty remembering the details, "She told me since I wasn't contributing to the household that I had to move out…that I was getting a freebee and that charity starts first with the family." I didn't know how heavy this burden was until I finally let it all go. My tears stung the corners of my eyes. Sitting doubled-over in the chair, thick moans left my chest as I wept with my whole body. It was my longest, deepest cry. Dr. Canes sat patiently, handing me tissue. I wiped my eyes and stifled my cry until I felt like I was in control again.

He looked at me and said, "You cry like a man. You cry like I do. Yeah, you gave a good, long, deep cry and then quickly choked it." He was right. And I realized that I was accustomed to doing this every time I cried. I never gave myself time to mourn. There never seemed to be time. I always had to "suck it up" and "be strong" so I could get work done—homework, college applications, etc. I treated myself like a machine, turning my emotions off to be efficient and turning my emotions on when it was convenient.

Dr. Canes invited me to come to a group session. I agreed to come, thinking that having group support might be good for me. People in the circle took turns telling their story. I listened thinking how funny it was that everyone needed counseling for such trivial issues. Then I stopped myself, realizing I was being too judgmental.

It was my turn, and I played my tape, "When I was 13, my house burned down. Then when I was 15, my mom passed away. When I was 18, I was kicked out of the house. And then four months later, my dad passed away." Why was it that by the time I mentioned my mom's death, I heard a huge gasp of pity rush in my direction. By the horror in everyone's voice, it was obvious to me that the students branded my experience as more tragic than theirs, making my initial assumption correct. Instantly, I became the center of attention, the object of everyone's pity, the standard they measured their tragedies against.

Whenever I saw some of these students on campus, they babied me and attempted to reassure me that, "Everything would be just fine." Despite their good intentions, I was annoyed by the presumptuous gestures and preferred they ignored me. I loathed pity from anyone. They weren't professional enough or mature enough to know what to do with my pain. The following Monday, I saw Dr. Canes when he said, "At the group session, I was worried about you. I wanted to hug you."

I smiled politely, "I'd rather not go back to the group sessions. I felt like the center of attention. I prefer only meeting with you once a week. Besides, being emotionally drained twice a week is too much for me."

"I understand. That's fine."

Dr. Canes helped me to grieve, and also helped me to rebuild my self-esteem. He began helping me to see how beautiful a person I was, by asking me, point-blank, "So how many times have guys flirted with you?"

"I don't know," I said. I didn't believe that guys, in general, had flirted with me; at least not around campus. Maybe one at UCLA, but to be honest, I wasn't sure. I was very stoic and out of touch with my sexuality; I could barely recognize if someone was flirting with me.

"I bet if I put a little birdie on your shoulder to see all the things you go through in a day, it would tell me how many guys look at you," Dr. Canes said as I became embarrassed. I guess Dr. Canes found it odd when I told him earlier that I was 21 years old and never had a boyfriend or been kissed before. I found it odd, too. I truly wanted to know what it was like to be in a romantic relationship. I watched my roommates find dates with ease and wondered what was so wrong with me that I couldn't even find one date. I never thought much about my looks, even though my roommates often told me I was pretty. I only knew myself as a young woman who had several unfulfilled crushes on different guys—most of them white, some Latino, and couple, Asian. Because of their lack of interest in me, I believed I must not have been too attractive. But, Dr. Canes tried to get me to see otherwise.

Later, he continued, "And, how often do you do things for fun?"

"Sometimes, I give myself a two-hour weekly treat to watch television. But that's it. I don't really have time.

Ever since I switched from being a math major to a civil engineering major, I have absolutely no time. I used to go to Interfaith, but I've decided to stop because I was there too much. Now, I'm studying all the time. If I'm not studying, then I'm either sleeping or eating."

"It's okay to go out. Be more social. Get involved in more social activities," he stressed, "Have a little fun."

By the following week, I was proud to report that I went out, "I went to a Hip Hop show for a couple hours last week. I watched a DJ perform. But I didn't stay for the whole thing because I had to study."

"Now, you didn't hurt yourself did ya?"

Slightly embarrassed at how stiff I was, I said, "No," smiling, looking at the floor.

There were only a few more sessions left. I began to count down the weeks—not because I hated meeting with him, but because I knew I would miss what these meetings did for me. I could think clearly and was much less fragile.

When the final week came, he said, "Well, Janet, this is it. You are strong young woman. You have really come a long way. I also think it would be a good idea if at some point you join a bereavement group so you can talk to other people who have lost loved ones."

"Yeah. I think so, too. I'd like that. Um, Dr. Canes, I want to thank you for everything."

18

Getting used to life without Interfaith was difficult. I went to class all day. Studied every night, even on Fridays. Studied all day on the weekends. Rarely socialized, despite doctor's orders. Every night before bed, I looked at the picture of Tuan and I taken at Interfaith—me, with a yellow rose and him, with bugged-out eyes as if he was shocked in the butt with a stun gun. I thought I'd never feel the Holy Spirit in the way I did at Interfaith. That frightened me, especially when combined with the possibility of not graduating and not finding friends I could trust and confide in. I stared at Tuan's wooden cross, remembering that my Catholic family missed me and kept me in their thoughts and prayers everyday. I prayed that the Spirit would still lead me, and that I would remain open to it.

‡

"Can I borrow your calculator?" I asked Devon, a guy sitting next to me at a physics tutoring session.

"Sure," he said, as he dumped his heavy backpack on the table. One by one, he took random things out of his backpack: a sandwich, some pens, a small plastic bag of mayonnaise. Then he found it, "Here it is!" pulling it out as a butter knife hit the table.

"Dang!! You got everything in there! Now, how ya gonna have a butter knife in your backpack?"

"So I can put the mayonnaise on my sandwich," he said matter-of-factly, holding up the tiny bag of mayonnaise. Within weeks, Devon and I became friends.

Devon had his own gang of buddies from the civil engineering department that I soon joined: Samantha, Rosario, Gerardo, Lina, Casey, Tim, and Jose. Lina sometimes called us a rainbow because the crew was Black, Mexican, Filipino, and white; every time she said this, the rest of the group just rolled their eyes with affection.

Devon was the most disciplined in the group: always prepared, always took notes, always did his homework, and always showed up to every professors' office hours. I don't think he ever went home; whenever I saw him, he was in the library studying. Otherwise, he was on the way to or from a class, carrying his massive backpack filled with all the major and minor provisions for the day.

Gerardo was the most brilliant and yet seemingly devoid of discipline. If there was a test that the rest of us studied a week in advance for, he studied the night before. He got an A while the rest of us got C's, D's and F's. This always frustrated us, but Gerardo remained humble, never wanting us to feel bad. That's just how he was. Once, he gave a clear explanation for something we learned in reinforced concrete class. We were so impressed, we said, "Ohh! Is that what that means?"

Shrugging his shoulders, Gerardo said, "I don't know, but it sounded good, didn't it." We laughed, and in unison Samantha and Rosario sighed, "Ay, Gerardo."

The rest of us tried being disciplined, but never got the grades the other two received. I tried hard, getting a lot of help from the others, but I just couldn't do it. I barely finished my homework and if I did, I was convinced my answers were wrong. My noble view of college as a spiritual journey, a fulfillment of my parents' wishes, no longer motivated me. Since I was on academic probation, the possibility of graduating was becoming unlikely. I was ready to be done with college and nearly ready to give up.

The director of the Women and Minority Engineering Program (W.M.E.P) had a friend who developed something called the Guaranteed 4.0 Plan—a system that could help students improve their grades. Devon, Samantha, and I started the study plan, reading through the packet of suggestions and charts: sit in the front row or the center row of the classroom, take bullet point notes of lecture and reading material, begin your homework the day it's assigned, review your bullet point notes whenever you have downtime, arrive at least ten minutes early to every class. I tried using every suggestion in the plan, and even bought a planner, like Devon's, to help me be more organized. I kept a schedule of my daily activities, detailing the amount of time I would spend on everything from studying for steel design class to eating dinner. I changed my diet and ate plenty of protein and fruits and vegetables; every morning I drank a "power shake" to get me through the day: a banana, avocado, raw egg, wheat germ, and orange juice—all blended at high speed.

Even though I had hope in all these changes, I still feared that everything would stay the same. It wasn't easy making these new adjustments; sometimes I wanted to revert back to my former ways because it was easier and familiar; besides, I wondered if I should try at all; what if I tried and failed again? I might not recover from it; I might become so disappointed in myself that I'd sink into a depression and permanently snap in half! So, why try if I'm only going to fail again? I'd rather just stay miserable, I thought.

However, being with Devon and his friends helped. They studied all the time—literally. Occasionally, they took brief breaks to celebrate someone's birthday, gobbling mouthfuls of cake and ice cream, watching the birthday girl (or boy) open gifts, then quickly returning to the books. We studied all day and night until the library closed at 11:00.

Once, Devon, Samantha, Rosario, Gerardo and I were on the fourth floor of the Science Library in one of the study wings. "Attention! The Science Library will be closing in five minutes. The Science Library will be closing in five minutes," a woman's voice warned over the loud speaker.

Rosario and Gerardo had already packed their books. Samantha and I started packing right after the announcement. Devon remained beneath the desk lamp, "Just give me five more minutes. I want to finish studying this last page. Just five," he begged.

"Ay, Devon!" Samantha said, "They already announced that the library is going to close. If you don't know it by now, you're not going to learn it in five minutes!"

He ignored her and kept studying. Usually, within a couple minutes after the announcement, an attendant inspected each wing to make sure everyone cleared out. No one came this time.

Samantha and I tried urging him, "Come on Devon! Let's go! The library's gonna close!"

"Done! Alright!" Devon said with satisfaction, throwing his books and notebooks into his backpack.

The main lights were off. It was dark and silent. The five of us walked through the empty floor and took the elevator downstairs. No one could stand up straight. We leaned on each other and on the elevator wall to keep from collapsing. The elevator doors opened, and when we approached the main entrance, the doors were locked. There was no way out.

The ultimate nerd predicament! Locked in the Science Library! With our bodies pressed against the glass doors, we flagged down anybody we thought could get us out, "Heeelp! We're locked in! Heeelp!"

Adjacent to the library was a study hall that was open until 1:00 a.m. We ran from the main entrance to the study hall and waved at the attendant, trying to get his attention. Not only did we get his attention, but at least fifty other faces also turned toward us, nudging each other, laughing.

He walked over to us. Pressing our lips in the crack of the door, we said, "We're locked in!"

"I don't have the key. Let me call someone who can unlock the main doors."

"Thanks," we said with relief.

A few minutes passed before a security guard came with the key and unlocked the door. "Oh, thank you, thank you. Thank you so much." We'd never been so happy...and so embarrassed.

Our relationship grew from that point on. We told this story over and over again, always agreeing that it was all Devon's fault. Our crew continued to study and laugh and celebrate birthdays and study some more; they pushed me to learn the material I was repulsed by and even got close enough to see how foul my temper could get; I made Devon and Samantha laugh with my stories, while they made me laugh with their jokes in Spanish; Gerardo and Rosario were family enough to wake me up from a nap so I could mediate one of their arguments; the gang celebrated my birthday (like my old roommates did) when all my relatives forgot; Lina taught me to sing early in the morning and be grateful for another day; I was afraid I wouldn't find the Holy Spirit outside Interfaith. I was happy to be wrong.

19

Tangled in the stress of trying to graduate and getting used to my new friends was still my experience at UCLA. As I became more aware of myself as a Black and Filipino woman, I also discovered all the things I didn't know about both cultures. I didn't know how to speak *Cebuano* or *Tagalog*. I knew what *Tinikling* was, but not *Singkil* or *Vinta*. I learned that Ferdinand Magellan had "discovered" the Philippines, but I didn't know that Opung Lapulapu killed him. I had heard about Jose Rizal but not Andrés Bonifacio. I knew Ferdinand and Imelda Marcos were corrupt, but I didn't know exactly how corrupt they were. In short, I knew very little about the basics in Filipino and Filipino-American history.

The few Filipinos that I knew as a child were those who were children of Mom's closest friends; some of them were also Black and Filipino. Being accepted by them never seemed to be an issue. I didn't have many Filipino classmates in elementary, junior high, or high school, but I was still proud to tell everyone I was half Filipino, mostly because people seemed to find me more intriguing. The few second generation Filipinos I met in college, with the exception of those I met at UCLA, were disconnected from their roots like me. The most we could do was share the memories of *lumpia* and *adobo*, imitate and laugh about the familiar, endearing sound of our elders' Filipino accents, and long for the day we'd return to our parents' homeland.

And as far as my Black side, I had the same problem. I barely knew anything about African and African-American history. I knew about slavery, Booker T. Washington, and Martin Luther King, Jr. That was it. I didn't know much about Africa prior to slavery, W.E.B. Du Bois, or Malcolm X. Didn't recognize names like Fannie Lou Hamer, James Baldwin, Audre Lorde, Lorraine Hansberry, Bayard Rustin, Mary McLeod Bethune, Gil Scott-Heron, or Mae Jemison. When I heard "African Diaspora" or the "Reconstruction Era," I didn't know what was meant. I didn't know what Kwanzaa was or why many African-Americans in college felt a connection to Egyptian mythology or a connection to countries in west Africa.

I was never completely comfortable with some of my Black sisters and brothers because I was insecure about my own Blackness; I was never sure if I was "Black enough." Often in the presence of other Black people, I felt I had to compete with them. This competitiveness took its origin in being the sole Black person in most of my social and academic circles. I learned to gain great satisfaction from being, by default, the "expert," a position expected of me by non-Blacks in my company. Many of these folks that I hung out with were the same people who tried using Black slang, acting animated around me, deeming me the "nice" Black person they could talk to, and addressing me as "sista" because they thought that was how they could effectively relate to me since I was a Black woman. And I just dismissed it all.

My need to compete could be traced to my choice to separate myself from other Blacks as early as the second grade. In elementary school, I noticed some of my Black classmates who didn't do their homework or got in trouble and made the decision not to associate with them so I wouldn't be labeled as "bad." I subconsciously put on the shroud of the "good Negro" which later evolved into an official uniform that helped me to assume the leverage to judge all of my sisters and brothers according to how they spoke, whether or not they smiled, how they dressed, and whether or not they were formally educated. I never knew that I was using the same standards of judgment and condemnation that some whites, Asians, and Latinos used to judge us.

The more I became aware of what I didn't know and the connection I didn't have with my people, the more difficult it was to learn what I was missing. What was holding me back? Embarrassment clung to every admission I made to not knowing my cultural histories. If other Filipinos discovered I didn't know who Lapulapu was, I knew I'd be judged. I'd embarrass myself if I began spending time at the Black Student Union, and people discovered I didn't know who Angela Davis, Marcus Garvey, or Maulana Karenga were. To save myself the public embarrassment, I avoided these circles and never placed myself in situations where I was a "learner" of my own cultures. I feared being vulnerable to criticism.

Because of this fear, I gravitated toward Mexican-Americans. Having friends like Shayra, Rosario, Gerardo, and Samantha influenced my language, my mannerisms, and my interests. I didn't necessarily seek them out because they were Mexican. They were just among the few people of color in the physical science and engineering department that I had met. They had not assimilated into mainstream white culture, but they weren't exactly militant revolutionaries either.

Being with them was comforting. My mother was an immigrant to this country like many of their parents. We understood what it meant to be the descendents of those in search of the "American Dream," and thus knew what it meant to be among the first in our families to graduate from college. With them, I was never held accountable for what I didn't know about my Black and Filipino backgrounds. Since I was not Mexican, there was never any pressure to be an expert in their Mexican heritage. I was free to learn without being stigmatized. And I enjoyed that luxury. However, something needed to change.

⚓

Thermodynamics always frustrated me. I flipped through the pages of the book as if reading a foreign language. Devon sat across from me studying diligently. He was wearing a black knit cap with the initials "N.S.B.E." on it.

"Devon, what's N.S.B.E.?" I asked.

"N.S.B.E. is the National Society of Black Engineers. It's a student-run organization divided into regions, each holding annual conferences. They have annual national conventions, too."

"What do you do at the conferences?"

"Oh, there so much fun. They have a lot of workshops on corporate environments and resume writing, things like that. There's a career fair where large corporations come to offer summer internships and information about their company. And a college fair…different colleges come to distribute information about their university. Oh, and roll call…I can't explain it…you have to see it. You should join and come to one of the conferences. I think you'd like it."

⚓

Thousands of Black people filled the convention center from wall to wall—skin tones from dark black to olive, eyes of deep brown to hazel, hair from relaxed to afros and dreads. As we walked passed each other, there was no fear, no hesitation…we were connected and it was only natural that we caught eyes and said, "Hello, my brotha. Hello, my sista," exchanging smiles and nods of acknowledgement…the way Da'y greeted other Black men when I was little. During roll call at the opening plenary session, the officers called out the names of each school, and instead of answering "Here" or "Present," the members of each chapter stood and sang chants (sometimes to the tune of Black sitcoms like the *Jeffersons* or *Good Times*) while the rest of the students sat doubled over in their seats, laughing, throwing their heads back, cheering on the group, eager to see what the rest of the chapters would do for roll call. After the session, stepping through the massive double doors of the ballroom, I found the career fair: corporations like 3M, Merck, and Anderson Consulting passed out souvenirs and pamphlets with information about their company and internship programs. Up the hall was the college fair where hundreds of universities like Cornell, Purdue, Prairie View A & M, University of Illinois at Urbana-Champaign, Georgia Tech, and Howard had representatives speaking to students individually about graduate school programs. I watched all the students walking past. Handsome brothas looked at me, while I snuck glances at them. The young men were dressed in dark three-piece suits and ties; the women wore smooth dress suits and heels; leather planners and briefcases replaced the 3-ring binders and backpacks used at school. Undergraduate and graduate students alike looked professional, carrying themselves with dignity: serious, but not aloof; confident, but not cocky.

I was in an atmosphere where all of us, as Black people, were college-educated and no one was made to feel ashamed; amongst each other, being smart was celebrated, not ridiculed. By admiring the beauty of my people across the room, I was admiring my own beauty. I had no reason to look at my nappy hair with contempt or disgust and no longer thought of my Blackness as the reason why boys weren't attracted to me. I was beautiful; and I was beautiful because I came from beautiful people.

I traveled from room to room, listening to speakers from the corporate world and academia who were eager to share their knowledge and experience. I absorbed the information, recklessly taking notes as they spoke about maintaining one's African-American identity in corporate America, making wise investments, studying U.S. history from an African-American perspective. They "talked back" to comments made about African-Americans often heard in corporations and universities like, "Yes, but are they qualified?" or "Well, we just didn't have 'any' apply for the job." With each workshop I attended, I understood why it was important to nurture and rebuild cultures that have been hated, questioned, ostracized, fetishized, and excluded from society. As I continued listening, I felt like I had arrived home without even knowing how far I had wandered away; many of these ideas crossed my mind, but I could never articulate them; hearing these presentations brought me so much relief and comfort that I wondered what sort of oblivion I had grown used to living in.

20

The computer lab was nearly full when I walked in. I logged into one of the computers and read an email from a friend:

Janeeeeeet,
You don't know how good it was to see these pictures you sent me (yes, I only received them today). Faces. One of the best things in life is just seeing pleasantly familiar faces. If there is any way that I can repay this favor, just let me know, I owe you one...Good luck, I'm sure you won't need it.

Peace,
Diego

Excited to finally hear from him, I typed my reply:

Hey there,
I'm glad you liked the pictures. I would have to agree that familiar faces are a gift. Oh! And about this repaying business...don't think of me sending the pictures as a favor that you must repay. There's nothing to repay. There's nothing you owe...Oh, and believe me...I will need the good luck in addition to many prayers, if you don't mind...You know I take back what I said earlier. I thought of a way you can repay me. Just continue to email and write to us little people here at Irvine, whenever you have time. This way we know you're okay. I know you

must have a pretty busy schedule, so I appreciate the time you spend replying.

Peaches and Cherries,
Janet

It had been a couple months since my friend, Diego, left for Harvard. We met the previous summer while working for a freshman women and minority engineering program. At the time he was working on his Master's Degree in mechanical engineering, but had recently been accepted to Harvard's History of Science Department to study Mesoamerican civilizations. As I sat at the computer and sent him that first email, I thought about how much I missed him: us traveling up and down the aisles of Albertsons' like two children, spending over $70 on refreshments for the opening night of the summer program; eating our burritos from Taco Bell, laughing and joking with our mouths full; us reaching our arms out as we walked passed each other on campus, gently touching hands, and Diego asking me like a little child, "Where ya goin'?"; me, after dark, knocking on his door to give him a journal wrapped in mint green parchment as a going-away gift; our first long conversation and me, for the first time in his presence, feeling butterflies in my stomach as I sat watching the room spin and slip into slow motion. By summer's end, I knew I had a crush on Diego. And I hadn't stopped thinking about him since.

We emailed each other once a week. Sometimes more. At the end of each day, I thought about what details and random thoughts I'd share with him next, knowing I could depend on him to always listen to and entertain my spectrum of ideas. After emptying those thoughts onto the keyboard, I checked my email everyday, eager to read his reply.

From the beginning, our emails were a mix of accounts of silly happenings, recipes, and philosophical, cultural, and religious assertions. Considering all the limitations a computer has, we used language to communicate our excitement, discoveries, frustrations, sadness, disagreements, spirituality, laughter, and care for each other. Over three thousand miles away, I saw him experience his first snow in Boston, playing "like a kid in a candy store" as he described it. And he could picture me, as I reminisced about my first snow with the kids in my old apartment complex packing snow in the stairs and sliding down on boogie boards.

I sent him a story emailed to me about a follower of God not giving up his "nature" to save a drowning scorpion that repeatedly stung him. When questioned, the follower of God argues that if the scorpion isn't giving up his nature to sting, why should he give up his nature to serve. I thought Diego would like the story. And then I sat down at the computer to read his reaction to it:

> Janet,
> …The story claims to use an example from nature to tell an ethical tale. My issue is that the system which constructed the tale is so far removed from nature that it probably thinks this a reasonable example. I know I'm reading too much into this, but the underlying point is the same. i.) Scorpions do not only sting, in fact they only do so when forced. Only someone who sees nature as inherently hostile would cast the scorpion in such a role. ii.) It is also the nature of man (even if s/he is a servant) to learn. How hard could it have been for the servant to figure out a different way to save the scorpion e.g. scoop him out towards the sand. To devote oneself to servitude and

adamantly refuse to learn seems to me more disservice.   iii) Assuming that this scenario could arise, is the servant really doing service to the species if s/he saves the scorpion? Wouldn't it be better evolutionarily for that scorpion to die and thus end the instincts which allowed it to get so close to the water in the first place?

Sorry if this is a bit abrasive or something, but I just finished reading some of T. de Chardin and his approach to religion represents to me most of what is bad about it. Anyway, how are you getting along in your classes? I really haven't heard from you in awhile...I understand completely that you're quite busy, I was just wondering.

Sigues la lucha,
Diego

It took me a few days before I could respond. I needed time to consider what he was telling me. I had no idea he'd have such a volatile response to the story.

Hi Diego,
...this is true. The story seems to imply that the only thing within a scorpion's nature is to sting (if we define our nature to be the essence of our being; our primary natural tendencies). At the same time the story also seems to imply that serving people is the only thing within human nature, but we know this is not true. The story leaves out a lot of things. It is highly simplified. However, I think it does this only to illustrate a point. I think that ideally, doing God's will (whatever that means), should be independent of the outcome as opposed to

doing good deeds (whatever those are) believing that God will reward us…

Regarding your second point, when you say learn…learn what? To learn not to do something when one gets hurt? To choose a different way of doing something in order to avoid getting stung? I think therein lies the point of the entire story. One can say that the man's intention was to continue to "save" despite the number of times he is stung. He attempts to save being aware of the risk involved…This would be good if all of us were invincible and could shake off pain as if it were nothing. But most of us cannot. We know that there is a limit to the good one can do— beyond this limit more harm than good can actually be done. But what is that limit? Or did God intend us to actually define a limit?

And about your third point, who's to say what would be better for the scorpion? Who's to say that the man was even "right" in making the attempt to save the scorpion? I think it is safe to assume that the man thought he was serving by saving the scorpion. How did he come to think of this? How do any of us come to believe that any good we do is actually good? I find myself asking this question countless times almost to the point where I don't even trust my "good" intentions. This is when I pray for the gift of discernment…praying that God will reveal to me through relationships, through books, through Scripture, the difference between that which is good and that which is not. It is good to ask questions and continue our search in an effort to understand who God is, but I think what it boils down to is prayer, faith, and trust…having to let go and let God…to be honest…I don't understand what any of this means at the moment. I am at a slump in my faith right now. I am still finding out what this faith and trust business is all about. I suppose I will be learning and relearning this lesson throughout the rest of my life.

Peace and more peace,
Janet

About a week and half later, he responded:

Janet,

Sorry, I can't really do justice to your response right now, but I did want to make a couple comments. Yes, I recognize that the story made some gross over-simplifications in order to make a point, but that is precisely my point; in simplifying, one must ensure that they have not been too selective…What I'm trying to say is that simplistic stories are easy to attribute meanings to, and even more so when one wants to believe in them. As long as one is aware of this bias then everything is kosher.

The other thing is that your argument seems to justify the wholesale slaughter of the Crusades and the invasion of the Western Hemisphere. You say that we must trust in our ability to serve and seek justification in prayer…isn't that exactly what the missionaries thought they were doing when they burned the Mayan texts, defaced their temples, destroyed the histories of all "pagan" civilizations with which they came into contact? This was my point about learning: if we come to a situation already "knowing" how to serve, then we dispose of an opportunity to learn. By assuming that he was saving the scorpion, he was serving only his own will and his interpretation of "God's" will, he gave no thought to how the scorpion might want to be treated. If he stopped and communicated with the scorpion, listened to it, tried to understand it, maybe he would proceed via a different approach...Oh yeah, thanks for the letter, I was cracking up: "be careful where you take a nap."

Keep the peace,
Diego

My argument justifies the "wholesale slaughter of the Crusades and the invasion of the Western Hemisphere!?" What? That's not what I meant! I was livid. And from thereafter, any time he spoke of the losses due to Catholic missionaries, I stubbornly resisted, attempting to prove to him, using my new and improved apologetics skills, that the Catholic Church has been guided by the Holy Spirit throughout the centuries and continues to possess the "fullness of grace." Becoming vehemently intent on converting him, I insisted on the righteousness of Catholicism. I knew that by defending "the Church" even though I was away from Interfaith, I was remaining faithful—doing my duty as a devout Catholic.

Nonetheless, he continued sharing with me all that he was learning about the goodness of Mesoamerican civilization. The importance of honoring one's ancestors. The value of humility. He spoke of his understanding of culture being that medium by which communities of people communicated with their Creator, with their environment, and with each other. He challenged me to think about whether or not a universal truth truly existed.

In one letter, he cleared up many misconceptions I had about Mayan civilization and explained in greater detail how important it is to listen to the community that one intends to "help":

> Janet,
>
> I'm saying that when you appeal to prayer and ignore the people in consideration, the result is much more likely to be in error. As you have said, prayer is not one hundred percent certain; sometimes we are unsure as to whether or not we are being given an answer. On the other hand, there are always external pressures which are giving us answers as to what we should do, e.g. politics, greed, power, etc. With the chance for error so great, shouldn't we make sure we take into consideration the very people we are attempting to "help"? That's what I'm saying...not that you are wrong in wanting to help, or that you are in the same position as the colonists, but that the implementation of Christian doctrine is more readily subject to misuse and so needs to be exercised with greater care. (I really would never say that what you are doing is "bad" because I don't believe it could be.)
>
> In reference to the Maya culture, there are a couple of general misunderstandings. First, in the 15th western century, the Maya had already left the large cities and were living in much smaller communities; communities not engaging in human sacrifice though still adhering to the writings of their predecessors. These were many of the texts which were destroyed. The Aztecs, with whom the Catholics first "witnessed" human sacrifice, were living in large cities, most notably Tenochtitlan. Now, if this practice were the sole justification for the attack on Aztec

culture, then the Catholics of the 15th western century were some of the greatest hypocrites of all time. Hadn't they just reinstituted the Inquisition, and can't we consider this to be human sacrifice? Indeed, those who did not believe in the Catholic faith were sacrificed so as to preserve the doctrine of the Church. Similarly, those who were captured in war from another Latin American nation were sacrificed for the order of society as the Aztecs had constructed. I'm not trying to say that either was right, just that they were the same and so now we cannot look back and say that the western invasion was ok because the natives were engaging in activities different from their own.

On the other hand, it seems that this one characterization has stuck with all Mesoamerican communities. Maybe the Catholics figured that since the Aztecs had engaged in human sacrifice, then so did all Mesoamericans...what other reason could they have for their actions other than gross (and erroneous) generalizations? All of this was justified to the Church at the time, and the conceptual basis for conversions in Christian culture in general have not seemed to change since this time, as witnessed by the "righteous right." Now, I'm not trying to lump all Christians together, just demonstrate the potential danger common to most.

Sorry I couldn't get more into Mesoamerican culture, but this was one point which I consider worth spending time on. Take care and good luck in winter quarter. (Have you started yet?)

Peace,

D

I listened, still defensive and skeptical. But I could not deny how deep Diego's sincerity and conviction ran; his thirst for truth and connection to his ancestors, profound; his emphasis on listening to the needs of a community, sincere. He taught me many things, and in spite of our disagreements, we remained ever interested in each others' deepest ideas and feelings. The intimacy of our thoughts and the chastity of our relationship made me fall deeper in love.

╬

As an early graduation gift, Lou bought me a ticket to Hawaii. This was perfect! It gave me time to rest and sort out my thoughts. And when I returned, I ran straight for the computer lab, excited to bounce my new realizations off the single man I knew would listen:

> Diego,
>
> I'm sorry it has taken me so long to reply. I have finally settled down after my "world tour." It was indeed restful, as well as enlightening.
>
> Hawaii was wonderful! I stayed at my cousin's home in Honolulu (while she was here on the mainland). She lent me the keys to her car and I was cruisin'!! The day after I arrived on the island, I filled the car with gas, bought a map, and drove. I can't recall a time where I had felt this carefree. Half the time I was driving, I had no idea where I was going. For once, in a very long time, the flowers smelled…nice. You begin to wonder why the flowers…the most beautiful of flowers…don't

smell sweet to you anymore. I used to love smelling the honeysuckle in Aldrich or listening to the birds sing. Then I stopped.

Gary once told me that we perceive the "daisies" as pretty when things are going well in our lives…then when life seems to not be so beautiful, we barely recognize that the daisy is there. Hmmm. It's funny. You know, I was beginning to believe that the flowers lost their scent, then I realized that I had lost my sense of smell… (to be continued)

Thank you for the "peace and hope,"
Janet

Three days later came Diego's response:

Janet,
I just wanted to let you know that I am listening, very intently in fact, but I don't want to say anything to bias you right now. I think I have an inkling of what you are going through…hence my silence. So please continue at whatever pace suits you best, and know that I am indeed listening attentively.

Regards,
Diego

I melted when I read his words. How could he know exactly what I needed to hear? I didn't reply right away. I called over Devon, "You have to read this Devon! Look at what Diego just wrote! I wrote him a letter a few days ago and this is what he wrote back. Isn't it sweet?" He squinted at the screen, reading the email, as I waited for his reaction. "Yeah," he said, "That's really nice. Wow."

"Okay," I said, "That's all I wanted to show you."
Devon just laughed and returned to studying.

And for the next five days, late at night when I was
all studied out, I began typing my epic:

Diego,

Over the last few years (and even
more so over the last couple of months), I have
been thinking and praying about what
happened to my sense of smell...how I can get
my sense of smell back. After muddling
through several reasons, I dismissed the whole
idea by saying: I am just burnt out. I need to
be in a different setting. Maybe then the
mental juices will begin to flow again. Indeed,
it will help to be in a different place...to gain a
fresh perspective on things. However, I fear
that one day I may take this reasoning to an
extreme...every time I get tired of something, I
will be reluctant to make use of what I have,
taking the initiative to change the situation I am
in (within my capabilities) and be more inclined
to just up and runaway (whether it be moving
to a different place or changing my major)...

...not that there is anything wrong with
running away once in awhile...but instead,
"running away" thinking that this is the sole
way of making any changes in my life.

Yes, I was (and still am) burnt out, but
I think another question I need to ask myself is,
"From what?" I'll answer this question by
telling a little story...

I remember my freshman and
sophomore year I was diligent and very
efficient...probably because I spent all my
hours studying and doing nothing else. Then

as I took classes outside of my major, became more involved at Interfaith and had some good conversations with people...I learned that there are other things that are important to me. Aside from learning about my love/need for other people (and not just my books) and other things, I learned that I need to take care of myself...taking care of my thoughts, my faith, my future, etc. A lesson that I learned very early on was to let myself cry when I needed to. I had become very good at telling myself, "I cannot cry now. I have work to do." I remember the morning my half-brother called to tell me that my father died. I cried a little bit. By afternoon, I found myself sitting at my typewriter, filling out an application for McNair that was due that day. People sometimes will drown their sorrows in work so they don't have to feel the pain. However, I don't think that was what I was doing. At that time in my life (3 years ago...wow...I make it sound as though it was ages ago), I took great pleasure in sitting and thinking about my parents. How funny they were. How warm they were. I didn't find reminiscing painful. However, I felt that it was too "time consuming"...

...so I stopped (well, I stopped when I could; there were times I didn't have that control...thank God). Now that I think about it, it seems that I have a history of cutting things out of my life in order to study. Despite all of the time I set aside for studying, I was still doing poorly in my classes. In part, I think I was burnt out from this...i.e. spending all of my time studying and not doing well, and leaving the quarter physically and emotionally drained. Last quarter was a prime example. I figured now that I am no longer involved at Interfaith, I can spend all of my time studying. "This time I will do well," I thought. But somehow I failed to figure in the time I would need to spend on graduate school applications/fellowships, etc. Come 6th week, I found that I nearly failed all of my exams…

…all sorts of thoughts ran through my head…not graduating, never continuing on to graduate school, changing my major, etc. For a very long time I had been wondering why I even continue as an engineering major. What am I working so hard for anyway? I'm not good at what I do. My grades certainly don't reflect that I am. Okay, what if grades don't truly reflect how well a person does know the material…can I say that I do know the material despite the ugly grades I have? My answer was no. I prayed for something to remind me why I was working so hard. Well, once again I found myself at my typewriter filling out applications when I didn't feel too good about myself nor the things which surrounded me. It was the GEM and FORD Fellowships…fellowships where you basically have to sell yourself (expressing your sales pitch with tact, of course.) How could I "sell" myself if I barely believe in what I'm doing and why I'm doing it?

As I was typing all the classes I've taken since '91 for the FORD application (which was a serious pain in the ass…excuse my language, but that was exactly what it was), I noticed my A's, my A+'s, A-'s and all of my B's. I kind of wondered how a person who had once done so well, could do so badly now. If I had the "juice" at some point in my life, it must be somewhere in my system today…it's just a matter of tapping into it.

Then Lina came in, with her normal cheery self, "Hey Miss Janet! What's shakin'!" I simply gave her a real sorry excuse for a smile. That's all I had energy for. Then I explained to her how stressed I was, etc., etc. Then my other roommate walked into the room and I cracked some sort of joke and we all laughed. Lina turned to look at me and said something to the effect of, "Wow! Despite the stress, you can still smile. I think it's your mom smiling through you." I agreed. "You know, I think she'd be proud. Both of your parents would be proud."

I thought about this. Then I remembered being with my mom in the coronary care unit. I was pointing out some detergent commercial on TV to her. I think my dad was sitting on the other side of the bed or looking out the window (at that time he was already sick). I can't remember. Anyway, I remember she turned to me and said, "You know, I won't even get to see you graduate from high school." Despite my desperate attempts to rid her of this thought, she repeated it again. She had reached a wisdom that was beyond my little 15 year old level of comprehension. She knew.

This was my little reminder of why I was continuing with the fight (sigues con la lucha, as you wrote once before…I think…correct me if I'm wrong.) She left the Philippines in hopes of eventually being greeted by a comfortable lifestyle here in the United States. Instead she was greeted by the Department of Social Services, an onion factory, and the Lancaster City Park where for two years aluminum cans had the privilege of being picked out of fresh trash by both her and her dark child.

She was later enrolled in some computer clerical training thing in Pacoima which, from what she was told, had a good success rate in terms of future job placement, etc. I think she was about a month to two months from graduating when she died.

So now I'm typing on the typewriter that she did her homework on every night. I'm her hope. She is why I fight. I believe I received the "reminder" that I prayed for.
I think I'll be finished tomorrow...

...something else I was thinking about was this line above. Ummm. It's always fun trying to guess the ways in which God speaks to us...answering our prayers. I cannot say that being reminded of my mother, etc. was the "reminder" that I prayed for...no questions asked. I can only say that I believe that it was. I'm a firm believer that i.) the Holy Spirit never leaves us and that ii.) the Holy Spirit speaks to people in several different ways. I've always known God to speak to me through the power of prayer (I apologize if I sound like a preacher). I'd like to elaborate on the first point in another message regarding the Catholic belief that the Holy Spirit never left the Church. You brought up some good points in one of your messages that I never addressed. I'll get to that when I'm through with this one. First, I'll give you a chance to absorb this message before I launch another bomb on you.

Well, to conclude I just want to say that I've made some changes in my life. I'd like to say the changes I've made are all a result of my "re-realization" of whose torch I'm still carrying (i.e. my mom's, even though this is definitely part of it). This would make my very long-winded story worthy of having a primetime drama made out of it. However, it wasn't that simple. It was a combination of things that have motivated me to change...change some very basic things in my life. I think for the most part, I was getting tired of feeling horrible about myself. I needed to take a strong, painful look at those things in myself, that I am responsible for, which have caused me to be dissatisfied with myself, so much that I begin to withdraw from people...because I am ashamed. (As well as the fact that I am now on academic probation...just a small thing I failed to mention.)

One of my biggest fears, as I think I mentioned, was for the sole source of my confidence to lie in my accomplishments and my knowledge. There are so many things that define me, not just what I do and what I know. There are my dreams, my hopes, my womanhood, my race, my faith, writing, whatever...the list continues. At various times during these last five years at UCI, I have taken time to develop in these areas. I am very happy that I did.

However, I feel I need to switch gears...I need to think about my career. If I want to become a professor, a good professor, I better have a good command of the material...which involves making adjustments to my current study habits, as well as, later on down the line. Since the institution of learning is so important to me (whether it be engineering or other things), I must admit, I do draw a substantial amount of confidence from what I know. So I looked and asked around for ways I could improve my study habits.

Luckily, at the same time I had reached this dilemma, a friend of the director of WMEP came to Irvine with the "Guaranteed 4.0 Plan" she developed. I know it sounds cheesy...but it's results are amazing...here are some suggestions from the plan: starting homework the day it's assigned, doing bullet notes for lecture and reading material, take 30 minutes/day to rest, see professors once a week...

It's been one week since I've made some of these changes. Let me just say that it is strange to be relaxed the night before a homework assignment is due and the memory retention is amazing. I know I sound like one of those infomercials. Oh, well!

Diego, I want to thank you for that kind message you sent to me when I first started this novel. Sometimes it is hard getting into all of the details in just one conversation, whether it be in person or via a single email message. I really appreciate your patience.

Janet

To share all of this with someone was special. To have someone listening was a gift. If becoming intimate meant having every aspect of my character, my idiosyncrasies, my daily routine known by another, then that was what I felt with Diego. He was listening; that was nearly all that mattered. Four days later, I received his response:

Janet,

I really want to thank you for sharing your thoughts with me. I wish I could do justice to anything you have said, but am afraid my talents (perhaps anyone's talents) are not sufficient. I would like to comment, if you don't mind, just very generally.

Speaking with a friend at dinner today, we somehow ran into the question of intelligence. One professor here, in particular, is unquestionably brilliant, but comes across as being relatively humble. It seemed to me then that there are really two types of approaches to being intelligent. On the one hand, some people realize that intelligence is a highly valuable tool for satisfying one's own desires, whether they be financial, intellectual, spiritual, whatever. These they pursue for personal gain. On the other hand, some recognize that substantial intelligence carries with it a significant responsibility, either to their own immediate community or an extended one. When to one course one commits, it is very difficult to switch to the other. Either one can be gratifying and self-propagate.

The trap which I think awaits those in the latter camp is that laid by the demon of cynicism. When one is committed to working for the good of a community, there are an infinite number of opportunities (temptations?) to throw up one's hands and claim that "it is not worth it." This is the burden, the "cross" if you will. In Mesoamerica, the concept was one of "cargo." Acts did not go without some form of reciprocal behavior, from activity in nature to that between families, or even within the home. Perhaps, this is a "cross" which has too often been ignored of late: the debt we must pay to our own families. It seems that we are constantly blaming our predecessors for something and never thanking them for allowing that one essential piece to persevere: hope. May your God keep and strengthen you, and maintain your hope.

Peace,
Diego

Reading his words, my feelings for him grew stronger. I knew, soon, I'd have to tell him how much I loved him. But, I could never write this in an email. I would have to tell him in person.

21

Making all those changes paid off. Despite my two quarters on academic probation, I concluded my undergraduate career on the Dean's Honor List my final quarter, finally graduating from U.C. Irvine in June 1996.

As I marched down the aisle, I couldn't believe that I was not only graduating, but was able to wear my gold chord from Chi Epsilon, the civil engineering honor society. Many of my closest friends and relatives, those who had supported me throughout my life, came to cheer me on: Anabelle, Gilberto and their daughter, Gabriella; Lou, Chera, and Mama Lila; Mr. Shepardson and his wife, Diana; Gina and her boyfriend, Lee; Gary, Ms. Weidemann, an old rollerskating friend, and one of my mother's friends. Although my parents could not witness my graduation, I felt them near. And I knew they were proud.

⚏

By September, I began working as an entry-level structural engineer at a steel company in Riverside. I had been waiting to live the "adult" life for a long time, and here was my chance. Being separated from campus with a "real" job made it seem official.

I rented a one-bedroom apartment not far from U.C. Riverside. It was furnished with no more than a futon and a desk. My kitchen table was a cardboard box; my refrigerator: a small orange ice chest; my bookshelves: old milk crates from a nearby grocery store.

When I first arrived, I bought a map and scouted the area by foot to find out what stores were within walking distance. Month by month, my apartment began to feel like home as I filled it with secondhand appliances and furniture: an old refrigerator for $50.00, Anabelle's kitchen table, and Gina's old couch. And I managed to buy a laptop on credit so I could journal and keep in touch with old friends. Having my own place was liberating.

Being the introvert that I was, I loved being alone. However, I missed living on a college campus with all the people around. I didn't have a community immediately nearby that I could trust. Finding friends and maintaining a social life took an extra effort.

I went to work and came home feeling completely empty and isolated. Gradually, a foreboding fear of death came over me—something I normally experienced during summers when I had nothing to do. Being constantly nervous, the only two things that gave me solace was picturing Diego in my daytime "him-feeding-me-grapes-beneath-the-tree-in-the-mist" dream and reading the school catalogues for the Jesuit School of Theology in Berkeley and the Harvard Theological School.

Holding a canister of pepper spray, I slept on the floor, worried someone might break in at night. In the morning, I went to work, ate lunch by myself, went back to work and then came home. Alone again. I was completed disconnected. Freedom and isolation found their meeting place.

I called Gary since he always knew how to make me feel better. "Well, have you ever read *Siddhartha* by Hermann Hesse?" he said, "It's a great book. This might help. But if this strange depression interferes with your ability to function, you need to take more serious measures."

As I read the book, I was captivated by Siddhartha's journey. While sitting beneath a tree outside the steel company, I reached the last few chapters, where the ferryman tells him, "The river has taught me to listen; you will learn from it too. The river knows everything; one can learn everything from it." I read on to find him saying, "...the river is everywhere at the same time, at the source and at the mouth, at the waterfall, at the ferry, at the current, in the ocean and in the mountains, everywhere, and that the present only exists for it, not the shadow of the past, nor the shadow of the future." These lines stirred up a longing for a timeless world—a desire to live an existence that extended beyond an ordinary 9 to 5 job. I needed meaning. I wanted a fresh beginning without the memories of the past shackled to my ankle.

While reading *Siddhartha*, I decided to search out a bereavement group—my first step toward a new start. For many years, whenever I initially met someone, I always ended up mentioning my parents' deaths. I knew that losing them forced me to develop certain skills and characteristics that I otherwise would not have, and I wanted people to recognize those strengths. However, I didn't want my parents' deaths to always be the first thing I spoke of. I wanted to stop depending on their deaths to prove I had strengths. I needed to let them go.

⌖

The first evening of the bereavement ministry, I was met by the soothing scent of vanilla candles. In the corner, resting on two chairs was an acrylic painting of heaven with Jesus waiting with open arms behind billowing clouds. I sat down at the table with the others. It was a small group, all women. The facilitators sat down and introduced themselves, "We'd like to welcome everyone this evening. I'm RayAnn Butler and this is Sandra Tyson.

Before we get started we'd like to ask all of you to please introduce yourselves and who died in your family."

As I listened, I noticed the others seemed more devastated than I. The deaths of their loved ones were fairly recent. One women lost her husband about a couple months prior. Another lost her spouse within the last year. The other woman lost her daughter to a drunk driver the month before. And then there was me, who lost both parents several years ago.

After the introductions, each person went into depth, telling their stories. When it came to me, I was slightly timid at first. I didn't use my dependable tape that kept me from crying. I just spoke, "When I was 12, our house burned down. We lost almost everything we had. We bounced from place to place and then my mom dies. I was 15. She died at 51 of liver cirrhosis and bleeding ulcers. I stayed with her side of the family for awhile, and then I was kicked out of the house. A few months later, my father dies. I was 19. He was 80 years old." I slowly felt the tension leave my body, as I continued, "Um, I almost didn't make it through college. I was on academic probation for awhile and then I finally graduated. But I still feel like a failure." When I finished and then listened to the others, I realized that I didn't really grieve for my mom until two years after her death. My tears before were mostly of self-pity.

Sandra and RayAnn then passed around workbooks, "These will be your journals. We encourage you to write down your thoughts over these next few weeks and record your progress." We opened them up, as they explained the various stages of grief. "Now, not everyone will experience all of these stages in the order," RayAnn said, "Some may not experience certain stages at all. However, it can still be a helpful model." I looked at the diagram they drew and saw the description of the last stage, "Embracing the reality of the deaths and letting go in order to continue living. Exploring new possibilities. Becoming more flexible. Taking more risks." I immediately recognized that that's where I was in life.

I left that night reflecting on what I shared. Seven years had passed since Mom died. Four years had passed since Da'y died. I was also dealing with other roadblocks in my scattered life: the house burning down, feeling like a failure, never feeling accepted by family. It's easy to say, "Pick up and go on with the rest of your life." What was funny was that there was a part of me that thought I was already doing that. Instead, I was carrying a magnet for more grief and disappointment, stumbling through life, functioning with it as if it were an organ. I had grown accustomed to preparing myself for the worst-case scenario, since the worst always happened anyway. I figured maybe if I was more prepared for "something bad to happen" then I could prevent it from happening or could at least save myself the disappointment. But, I couldn't, and this magnet for pain became just too heavy to carry.

When I came home that night, I cried so hard; even harder than when I was with Dr. Canes. Feeling my eyes burning, I snatched breaths between each weep. And that night, I had my deepest sleep in seven years. Whatever seized my body released me during the course of the night; in the morning, I felt cleansed. Later, I had a vision that all the things that were once difficult for me would come with ease: I would be able to read faster, socialize with strangers without inhibition, find peace and stability, and know exactly what I wanted in life. It was a clear vision. I laid prostrate in disbelief, yet ready to begin again.

⊹

It was a good time to do all the things I couldn't do during my final year at Irvine. I decorated my apartment, hanging up my "Life's Little Instructions," a giant wooden rosary, and a rose stone carving of Mary and Jesus, all the while imagining conversations between Diego and I, singing along with Mary J. Blige as "Real Love" played in the livingroom. I spent hours in the kitchen cooking all the dishes Tatay used to make. And when I finished, I listened to KPFK, being exposed to the politics I was interested in but never heard about in the mainstream media: issues mostly concerning race, gender, and sexual orientation. Throughout the week, I devoted time to building up the St. Andrew's Newman Fellowship and establishing an African-American reading group at U.C. Riverside.

I was happier, however, I didn't feel completely fulfilled. Riverside was so desolate and lifeless and disconnected. I longed to live somewhere else. Like San Francisco or something! For weeks, I walked to a local coffee shop, writing in my journal, reading, drinking mochas, and pretending I was someplace in the Bay Area.

After Gina and her boyfriend, Lee, helped me buy a car at a nearby car auction, I was no longer restricted to my little corner of town. I often drove to the other side of the city to another coffee shop with live jazz music and a classy, smooth atmosphere. I came in to buy my usual orange spice tea and write in my journal, still daydreaming about the Bay—a place that seemed to fit my romantic image of vibrant city life. I was called to be somewhere that had poetry readings and museums and plays and modern dance performances. Someplace that was diverse across racial and sexual orientation lines. I wanted to make friends with people from all sorts of social circles—with people who didn't live at the mercy of superficial desires and hollow pop culture. I also needed to recommit myself to God and be in the presence of others who desired the same.

At work, I was making photocopies when I began thinking about how impersonal my work environment was. Whose life was I really affecting? Does my work have any personal impact?

"I want to be connected to something eternal," I thought, not exactly sure what that meant. But the desire translated into a need to be connected to the outside world, hoping to find my greater purpose. I needed to extend beyond the confines of my job, my apartment, and Riverside and go even further away than Northern California...

Like...Boston. Yes, Boston. Why? Three words: Diego was there. Boston could possibly give me a hint of what life was waiting to give me. Most definitely, it would also be my chance to finally tell Diego how much I loved him.

22

October 8, 1996, I flew to Boston. I was nervous when I knocked on the door of the dance studio where he asked me to meet him. It opened and there he stood, just as handsome as I could remember. Diego's black hair was long, reaching his shoulders. His mahogany skin and bright smile brought back memories of the summer we worked together.

"Hey, Janet, how are you?" Diego said, as he hugged me.

"Great!" I said stumbling in with my suitcase.

"Well, right now we're in the middle of doing a ritual dance. You can sit right over here. We'll be done pretty soon." I sat and watched as Diego and the other students performed a ritual in the tradition of their Aztec ancestors. They danced in a circle, chanting. Later, they sat down on the floor in a circle with the four elements at the center; they gave thanks for each one: their eyes closed, their bodies still, their energy focused toward the center. Their reverence made me feel they were transcending this life. I looked away and remembered how hard I tried to convert him no more than a year ago. My image of God was broken and rebuilt into something far more fluid and inclusive. Tears welled up in my eyes when I realized how God was much "bigger" than my narrow conception of Him (or Her). I was embarrassed at the thought of my arrogant attempts to convert him. How ironic it was that I was converted instead. I could no longer in good conscience believe that there was just one religion that embodied the ultimate truth. There had to be many ways of truth that lead to salvation or eternal life or enlightenment.

To ignore what I was witnessing and all that Diego had shared about his culture would be to ignore an opportunity to learn—what Diego had long tried to explain to me.

In an old, navy blue truck, we left for his apartment so he could take a shower and change. I sat in the livingroom, waiting, drinking guava juice. We talked for a little while before deciding to eat at a diner up the street.

We took our seats at this restaurant that reminded me of Mel's Diner. "So how have you been? What have you been up to?" I said.

"Well, I took a trip to the Yucatan and visited one of the temples there. I pretended to be doing research so I could go up to the top after dark. It was beautiful. I was so overwhelmed by the beauty of the stars and the sky that I danced, paying homage to the sky and my ancestors."

The excitement in his voice and eyes made it seem as though a part of him was still atop that temple. His spirit moved me; the way he told his story reinforced all that I witnessed and felt earlier that morning.

Our conversation lasted at least two hours at the diner; he talked about the work it took to organize the Latino community at Harvard; we spoke of what we loved most about Cornel West; he described what it was like to sit in one of Dr. West's classes, "He's so brilliant, he said, "It seemed like his brains oozed out of his ears!" And when we finished eating, we left to take a walk around Harvard.

Diego and I walked aimlessly across campus and Harvard Square, roaming up and down the streets, passing bookstores and novelty shops. As we approached a wide lawn near the center of campus, I stopped and looked around.

"What are you doing?" he said, staring at me.

"I can't believe I'm at Harvard," I said, standing in a daze.

"Hah, hah," he laughed, "Come on. Let's go."

We walked a little while before I asked him, "So, when someone asks where you go to school, what do you tell them?"

"Well, I don't like to tell people that I go to Harvard," he said modestly, "I might start off by saying I go to school back East. If they persist, I'll say I'm a graduate student. If they still persist, I'll say I'm a doctoral student. Lastly, I'll tell them that I go to Harvard." I was impressed by his modesty, finding him even more attractive.

"You know, I have to tell you that it's been great emailing back and forth. Your emails give me a good springboard that help me articulate and test out my ideas," he said.

"Yeah. They've done the same for me," not knowing what to say, feeling heat rising into my cheeks.

Then the moment finally came when I couldn't hide it any longer, and I said, "Diego, I have something to tell you." He turned to face me, sensing the seriousness in my voice.

"Over the last few months of emailing," too embarrassed to admit that it was much longer than that, "I have grown to like you. I like you a lot."

He was in shock. "I don't know how to respond to that," he said.

"You couldn't tell?"

"No, not at all. Uh, this is quite a bomb you're dropping on me. I don't know what to say. I'm flattered. But I don't think things can work out. I'm not really ready for a relationship right now."

Someplace where I couldn't feel its beat, my heart sank down deep within me. Everything said thereafter melted into a muffled sound getting caught and tangled in the cacophony of traffic noise and the conversations of strangers. I was quiet. Diego continued to talk about random things that I paid little attention to; I suppose he was trying to break the tension, but he only drove me crazy.

Later that evening, he dropped me off at the airport. While waiting to check-in, I stayed quiet, not wanting to cry. As he twirled the cushion on the handle of my suitcase, I was reminded of his childlike manner and was disappointed that once the night was over, I would no longer share that playful side with him.

Crowds of people rushed past to catch flights and find their baggage. We weaved through as we approached the gate. I hugged him, "Goodbye, Diego. Thanks for everything."

"Goodbye," he said. I turned my back and walked toward the gate. My pride clenched my tears until that first step away from him. And then they ran slowly, stinging the corners of my eyes, streaming down my cheeks, meeting below my chin where I wiped them away. As I waited for my plane, I squirmed in my seat trying to keep from drawing too much attention. I cried while waiting at the gate and throughout the entire plane ride home, thinking myself foolish for actually believing I'd come home being his girlfriend.

23

When I returned, the signs were obvious that the steel company would soon go out of business. The company received frequent notices from the IRS to pay its back taxes. Clients called everyday complaining about unmet deadlines. And we, the employees, often went more than a month without pay.

After taking great pride in being independent, I began having trouble paying my bills and wasn't sure where to turn. I began to think of other young people fresh out of college who had the emotional and financial support of their parents to fall back on; when Mom and Da'y died, I lived without that security because I had no choice.

Then I remembered when Diana, Mr. Shepardson's wife, surprised me one afternoon during the previous summer, saying, "Janet, we know you don't have anyone to be your safety net. We want to be your safety net." At the time, I didn't know exactly what that meant, but I knew it felt good. Amidst the "amount past due" notices and the phone calls from creditors, I learned what they meant, and turned to the Shepardsons to bail me out. Then, within a few months, I was reduced to part-time and needed to find another job if I wanted to eat and pay rent.

In the office, when I was supposed to be estimating the amount of steel in the latest project, I called all the Catholic schools in Riverside, asking if they had any positions available for math teachers. After receiving several no's, I found one that had an opening.

I came in for an interview, and was immediately asked to cover for a teacher who would begin chemotherapy soon. For the next six months, I substituted four classes—5th through 8th grade math.

I never imagined myself teaching elementary and junior high school students. And when I stood before my first class, I can't say that it came naturally. I was plain and rigid. I was a social prune after spending my final year of college staying in libraries all day trying to graduate, without the benefit of socializing at Interfaith. Now here I was, speaking and being "on" for four hours a day, sweating and panting by the time my last class left the room.

Gradually, as the weeks passed, not only did the students force me to get used to being vocal, but they also broke through my reserved shell, making me smile and giggle as I saw thank you notes and stickers with bunny rabbits and puppies on my desk, found Easter baskets and chocolates in my mailbox from parents, and outsmarted my students who tried hiding my teacher's manual.

At the same time, the longer I stayed, the more concerned I was about the 8th graders. Many of them were labeled as "bad" students or "the ones you have to watch out for" or students who weren't "goal-oriented." By looking around, I never saw any teachers that would give them a reason to be goal-oriented. Although some may have been well-meaning, I found none of them inspiring. Watching the other teachers, I wondered what they were teaching the students to become. Through the discipline and the manners they were taught, they were being conditioned to be accepted by an elite class of people within society—trained to be good, obedient, little citizens who would never question authority. When it came to religion, they were taught how to go through the motions of saying the "Our Father" and the "Hail Mary," but they didn't have a sense of what spirituality was. The students, particularly the 8th graders, didn't fit the mold. They were the ones who loved everything from Hip Hop to punk music—the skaters, the graffiti artists and everyone in between; the ones who in spite of their pimples, their cracking voices, and their inability to do basic pre-algebra, were convinced they were the coolest kids at school. Their hormones were raging, but they had to share a campus with elementary school children. These kids needed wisdom that they could take with them to high school and into adulthood. Exactly, how this would be done, I didn't know. All I knew was that I understood and enjoyed their rebel spirits, since I hated imposed social norms, too.

I suppose through my teaching style, the clothes I wore, and the stories I told, the students identified me as someone who was different—someone who might not be so bad. Once, a student asked me, "Ms. Stickmon, do you smoke?"

I said, "Uh, no. Why?"

"I dunno. You just seemed like someone who'd smoke." Instead of launching into my usual tirade about how smoking doesn't make anybody cool, I just smiled, finding it funny that I, as a person who detested cigarette smoke, was viewed as a smoker. Nonetheless, by their excitement to come to my class, even when they didn't know what they were doing, told me I had their attention and respect.

These 8th graders were outgrowing their school and something needed to be done to maintain their interest in their education. I noticed they needed extra help with algebra, but the 50-minute classes weren't enough to give them the help they needed. I could hold Saturday tutoring sessions at the city library, I thought. But, they'd need an incentive. McDonalds! Yes, after tutoring, we can all go to McDonalds to hang out and socialize. My appeal to them was, "After we work hard, we can play hard." The rest was up to them.

On the first Saturday, six to eight students came. The following Saturday, my entire class came—all fourteen students. Some were dropped off by their parents; others arrived on their bikes; two showed up on skateboards.

The students had their questions ready and we worked through the problems one by one, minds concentrating, veins bulging, sweat dripping. I jumped from table to table answering all of their questions. Some questions were too difficult to answer in one breath, so I sat down to figure those out with them.

"Ugh! I hate problems like these," I mumbled to myself.

"Hah, hah! Wow! You're actually doing the problem with us. Cool!" a student said.

I smiled and kept working on the problem, eventually understanding why they had so much trouble with it.

When we were done, the students closed their books and left for McDonalds with smiles on their faces. "Math has never been that fun. I actually understand it now!" one said, while a few others agreed, "Yeah, yeah. I like math now."

It was difficult to know who was having more fun—me or the students. Learning about them outside the classroom didn't feel like work. And bringing them to McDonalds didn't feel like an activity I was chaperoning. It was a chance for me to get to know them and for them to get to know me. When we sat with our cheeseburgers and French fries, talking candidly about friends and dress codes and conformity and sex and abstinence, I learned how bright and insightful they were. They were young adolescents who had been treated like children, being told what to think, what to say, how to say it. Indeed, they were in search of direction, but they also wanted someone to listen to them.

The more I learned about them on Saturdays, the stronger our relationship as a class became; and the closer I became with all my students, the more I was in awe of how rewarding teaching could be. However, teaching math for the rest of my life wasn't for me. Theology was my love. Perhaps, I could teach theology.

24

In February 1997, I went to the Anaheim Religious Education Congress. I stayed in the arena for hours, marveling at the thousands of Catholics in the room. I walked around looking at the different booths and displays: Homeboy Industries, Liturgical Press, the Jesuit School of Theology in Berkeley (J.S.T.B.). There it was! That was the school I had been reading about for almost a year.

I approached the booth, but noticed there was no representative there. I kept walking and went around to the next aisle and saw the Franciscan School of Theology (F.S.T.), which was also in Berkeley. I had never heard of this school, so I decided to ask a few questions. On a red carpet, there was a beautiful display with brochures, flyers, and pictures of students. A tall man with a gentle manner was tending to everyone.

"Excuse me," I asked, "What degree programs do you offer?"

"We have the Master's of Divinity, the Master's in Theological Studies, and the Master's of the Arts," he said.

"What about G.R.E. scores? Mine might be fairly low."

"Don't worry. In the Master's in Theological Studies Program, G.R.E. scores aren't required. Don't worry about it. Here's an application," he said, handing it to me, "You should apply. What was your name?"

"Janet Stickmon. What was yours?"

"Dean, Dean Wilson. I'm in charge of student recruitment."

"Thank you, Dean. I'll go ahead and apply. Thank you so much," I said, beaming.

A door just opened up. This was perfect timing since I would be out of a job soon. I wasn't quite sure what this opportunity would lead to, but I knew something great was happening.

I wasted no time asking a couple priests and my spiritual director for letters of recommendation. By the time I received them, I finished writing my essay and filling out the application. On April 2, 1997, I mailed it along with a loan application to F.S.T.

I waited. And waited. Weeks passed. Then Dean called, "Hi Janet, you've been accepted into F.S.T. However, about that loan, I'm afraid you didn't qualify."

"I didn't? Well, what can I do?"

"Don't worry. Something can be worked out. We won't let money be the reason you can't come. I'll be in touch with you."

Shit! I won't get the money. I'm not getting in. Preparing for the worst, worrying that my calling into theology school and out of engineering was about to be quenched, I became infuriated with God, "Why did you bring me this far just to disappoint me? Were you stringing me along just to watch me get excited?!"

I waited.

And waited.

Dean called again, "Hi Janet. I wanted to let you know that the school can offer you a loan. But you need to come here in person for an interview. For certain you will get it. And also I found an apartment for you. All you'll have to do is pick up the key. It's official. You'll be attending F.S.T."

I couldn't believe it! My dream to be in the Bay Area was about to come true.

With the help of people from the steel company, I packed and loaded my belongings into a Uhaul truck and began my drive to Berkeley.

On the way, I drove to Anabelle's house to say goodbye to her, Gilberto, and their 5-year old daughter, Gabriella. When I arrived, I sat at the kitchen table and took out a couple of friendship bracelets from my backpack.

"Gabriella, I have something for you." She walked over to me with her long, brown hair and peaceful, little face.

I tied each bracelet around her tiny wrists. "Gabriella, I'm going to be moving a few hours away. I won't be as close as I usually am. I'm giving you these bracelets so you'll always know I'm thinking about you," I said, as the tears rolled down my cheeks, "Please, don't ever forget me. I won't forget you. Okay?"

She began to cry before wrapping her arms around me. That was my baby. I was there at her birth. I held her when she had earaches. I taught her how to do the sign of the cross before the altar, pointing out Jesus on the cross. I watched her grow during her first five years in this world; I was going to miss her. I was going to miss the whole family. They were among the few relatives on Mom's side that treated me like family. Being so far away from them would be difficult.

After hugging the three of them goodbye, Anabelle quickly snapped pictures of Gabriella and I in the Uhaul. Then at 6:30 a.m., I left for Berkeley; just me and everything I owned. I was off to a new start and felt free. When I looked out the window, what fallow land I saw bore nothing but possibility. I couldn't wait to see what was waiting for me in Berkeley. Passing cows and rows of orange trees and garlic, I sang to myself, praying between songs that I'd have enough money to pay for gas.

About seven hours later, when I reached the 80 Freeway and saw signs for San Francisco, Berkeley, and Oakland, I became excited. I turned on the radio, found the station that sounded like *The Beat*, and started listening to KMEL. I exited at University Ave. and maneuvered through busy traffic. I was finally in the Bay Area.

When I reached the apartment building, I parked in the driveway and climbed out. A slender, slightly bald white man with an earring came out the front door.

"Hi, do you by chance know where apartment #203 is?" I asked.

"Oh yeah! That's right across from ours. Hi, I'm Andy," he said, reaching to shake my hand.

"I'm Janet. Nice meeting you. Um, where do you think I could park my truck?"

"You can park it behind the building," Andy pointed, "That'll probably be best."

As I squeezed the truck through the driveway and behind the apartment complex, Andy rushed upstairs calling out to his wife with excitement, "Hey Gedera! Guess what?! There's another person of color moving into the building!"

I went to F.S.T. next door to pick up the key and went to my apartment. When I returned, there were two young men near the stairs barbequing and drinking beer.

"Hi! Are you a new tenant?" one said.

"Yeah. I just moved into #203."

"Oh really? I used to live in that apartment. My name is Ron."

"And I'm Tim," the other man said, holding his beer and flipping over the chicken on the grill.

"I'm Janet. I just drove up from Southern California."

"Oh yeah! Whereabouts?" Ron asked.

"From Riverside."

"Wow! Well, hey, there's gonna be a barbeque this week, on Friday or something. It's for all the tenants. You have to come."

"Sure, yeah, I'll be there. Thanks. I'll see ya there…Well, I'm gonna go unpack. Nice meeting you," I said, walking upstairs, thinking about how goodlooking they were, especially Tim.

When I walked into the apartment, the sunlight brightening the room, I noticed it was much smaller than my old place. It was a studio with plenty of windows and a giant hole in the carpet staring at me from the center of the livingroom/bedroom/familyroom. I immediately thought of my multicolored rug that was just big enough to hide the hole from guests. After a couple tenants helped me bring some boxes in, I unpacked, looking at my new place in disbelief: I was finally in the Bay Area, in Berkeley. And for my first two weeks there, I lied awake at night, pinching myself, wondering if it was all real.

Later, at the welcome barbeque, I got acquainted with my new neighbors, Gedera and Andy. Mid-conversation I learned that Gedera was Peruvian and originally from New York. Her and Andy met in Southern California and had been married for a few years.

"Yeah, we met while we were in InterVarsity," Gedera said.

"Hey, I used to go to InterVarsity meetings while I was at Irvine. I used to be a part of a group called Catholic Presence that had members visit each of the Protestant fellowships…so we could learn more about each other."

"Wow! Yeah, we were in InterVarsity for a long time. Then, when Andy began studying Biblical languages, he left Christianity and became agnostic. He'd come home and share the things he learned. Pretty soon, I stopped being Christian, too."

"Oh, really?" I said, fascinated but confused.

"Yeah, after studying scripture in Hebrew and Greek," Andy said, "I discovered just how flawed this text, taken as revelation, truly is. I couldn't continue being a Christian in good conscience, not after what I'd learned."

I nodded politely, despite my confusion. I thought the deeper you studied theology or Biblical languages, the deeper your faith in God became. I wondered what exactly he learned, but didn't ask any questions. I became uneasy at the thought that I might lose my faith, too.

╬

The Franciscan and Jesuit schools weren't the only places one could study theology in Berkeley. Nine theology schools—six Protestant and three Catholic—together with the Center for Jewish Studies, the Institute of Buddhist Studies, and several other centers affiliated with the consortium made up the Graduate Theological Union (G.T.U.). Most of the schools were located in what some called Holy Hill, an area on the north side of U.C. Berkeley. And when I first stepped foot on Holy Hill, its serenity invited me to stay: majestic trees towering over the streets, spider webs catching auburn pine needles in the bushes, leaves of pale yellow and jade green falling to the ground to mingle with lavender petals from nearby blossoms, the scent of pine and jasmine and the aromas of freshly cooked meals and clean laundry from surrounding apartments.

In the morning, I went to the opening Mass and orientation, discovering more about this Holy Hill. I chose my classes and began asking myself questions about my vocation in life. I knew I had been called by God to do something great in the Catholic Church. I was in the company of clerics, the religious, and lay people all serving God in some type of ministry. Was my calling to become a nun? I thought about it briefly, only to dismiss it, finding marriage more appealing. I tossed around the ideas of pursuing interreligious dialogue, liberation theology, gang ministry, and pastoral counseling. Was I called to be a preacher, teacher, pastoral associate, counselor, or a priest (when the day would come)? Whatever I'd become, I wanted to be animated and vibrant—a part of a new generation of Catholics—a progressive generation both in ideology, as well as style. I intended to make Catholicism understandable and palatable to those in my generation and younger. What came to mind was a scene from *Keeping the Faith*, where Ben Stiller and Ed Norton walk down a busy sidewalk in slow motion with their sunglasses and black leather jackets. They looked hot and appealing! But the scene depicted more than just the image of a "cool" minister; it represented ministers who were *of* the world, not above it. I, too, wanted to be in touch with reality and not cut off from the world. To become more aware of God's presence, I couldn't embrace an escapist mentality; to truly know Him or Her, I had to be in the midst of humanity, dealing with conflicts, dealing with pop culture, and dealing with social structures, and not escaping from any of it.

At the same time, I was aware of my unusual capacity for listening to the tragedies of others and wanted to use this gift somehow. Over the years, friends, roommates, family, strangers, all voluntarily shared their most intimate details with me. Never overwhelmed by their stories, I listened and asked questions to help them make more sense of their situation. I never sought out "miserable" people or took pleasure in the misery of others. Somehow people who needed to talk just found me. What seemed strange was that it took very little for someone to begin opening up to me. I never prodded my friends or acquaintances when I suspected something was troubling them. And I didn't pretend to be disinterested or apathetic either. If they began to talk, I'd show my concern, but I'd never initiate the conversation in fear of appearing too presumptuous—believing as if I was entitled to knowing their business. People felt free to talk around me and I listened. When it seemed that this gift had its place in ministry, I regularly asked God to reveal to me how I could use it. And then I was led to the Franciscan School of Theology.

⫟

The G.T.U. was a different world. Students greeted their professors by first name. Professors like Sr. Eva Lumas, Fr. Eddie Fernandez, Fr. Ibrahim Farajaje, Sr. Mary McGann, and Fr. Kenan Osborne were extremely approachable, treating their students with genuine respect— a far cry from my experience with many professors at U.C. Irvine.

And age. Age seemed irrelevant. Though I was young and less experienced than many of my classmates, I was treated as an equal. And by watching professors, especially, Sr. Mary and Fr. Kenan, I'd swear they were unaffected by time. They were animated and energetic in the classroom; playful and warm like children. In their presence, I never feared growing with age.

And witnessing ministers (classmates and professors) be completely human, without their "pastoral" faces on, was fascinating. Seeing them wear jeans, dance at parties, and be on a first name basis with each other tripped the hell out of me! They desired to be free—free to laugh, dance, smoke, shop, cuss, cry, be angry, workout, embrace their sexuality, or have an occasional drink at a bar without being judged as less than holy. To the general populace, these things seemed out of character for a priest, sister, brother, or lay minister because the public often projected inflated views of purity and unattainable standards of character on them. Ministers sometimes got tangled in these projections, finding themselves operating from a persona that others had shaped for them (and sometimes partially shaped by themselves), hiding their most authentic selves as not to scandalize their congregations.

Being in the company of other ministers and becoming friends with them, I discovered how important it was to have a group of friends that one could relax with, be candid with, vent with. Without such support systems, I could become burnt-out and isolated, measuring my self-worth only according to how much I served others. I didn't want to end up living my whole life from a rigid, predictable persona, only to realize I barely recognized myself and barely helped those I intended to reach out to.

My greatest fear was becoming the type of minister I occasionally saw—the one who mistook a fake sense of holiness for the real thing; a person who knew how to play the part, but didn't know how to love. I feared becoming some person who didn't reflect my true self, being so isolated in my relationship with God that I wouldn't know how to relate to the average person. I thought about Jesus: God loved his people so much that God poured Godself into human form, speaking and living the human language so humanity could better understand God. Jesus was a human being that felt every feeling from anger and hopelessness to utter joy. That was the way I wanted to be human; and that meant being honest with myself—

acknowledging and embracing everything about me, all the time.

╬

Late one afternoon, I ran into Ron while walking to the library.

"Hey, Janet! How are you?" he said.

"I'm fine. What's goin' on?" I asked.

"I'm waiting for this priest from Tanzania. We're supposed to have dinner, but he's about an hour late."

"He'll show up," I reassured him, having no real idea if he would or not.

About a week later, I went to a party at the Franciscan School. With champagne glasses and hors d'oevres in hand, everyone mingled, meeting new people and catching up with old acquaintances. A man in the doorway was looking around, smiling. "Hi, I'm Janet," I said to him, reaching to shake his hand, "I'm a student here at F.S.T."

"I'm Richard. I'm visiting here from Tanzania. I'm a priest and came here to work on my doctorate."

"Tanzania? Were you by chance supposed to have dinner with a guy named Ron?"

"Yes! Yes, that's my friend!" he said excitedly.

Little did I know that we'd soon become friends. Richard lived just up the street from me, and whenever I felt like talking or watching television, I walked to his house. At times, I ran to him in tears, searching for advice. Then as the months passed, he began bringing me his frustrations, as well.

"You know, it's strange. I have a lot of women who hit on me...sexual advances," he laughed, "Goodlooking women! Sometimes they stroke my leg or even leave me keys to their houses or to their cars. You know it can be very hard, Janet," Richard sighed. Immediately changing his tone, he continued, pointing his forefinger to the heavens, "But I have always been faithful to my vocation as a priest. It has been hard. But, sixteen years and I have never broken my vow of celibacy."

"They know you're a priest, right?" I said in awe that he was telling me all this.

"Yes!" he said, as my mind filled with questions, wondering how many other priests might have similar experiences. What makes women so attracted to them? Do they represent the ideal man…someone who is warm and giving and gentle? Are they drawn to them because priests represent the unattainable? Are women attracted to them because they might be the only men who take time to listen to their needs? And why was Richard telling me? Was there no one else he could tell?

⊥⊤

"Be careful. Many people will come to you looking for answers," said Gloria Loya, my professor for *Pastoral Counseling and Inculturation*, "It's important to understand that that is not your job. You need to understand a person's worldview…assisting the person to look at all of the circumstances involved in a situation. Then you can help the person help themselves arrive at a resolution."

As she spoke, her gentle, yet intense spirit captivated me. Gloria belonged to the Presentation Sisters of the Blessed Virgin Mary (P.B.V.M.). "P.B.V.M really stands for Pretty Brown and Very Mexicana," she'd always say. When she spoke about cross-cultural pastoral counseling and her experience as a Mexican-American woman, her depth of faith and connection to her people held my attention.

Sitting in class, listening to her words, I thought about all the people I had trusted in the past, and all those people that trusted me. For the first time, I felt the weight of how crucial it was for me to be a good pastoral counselor, paying close attention to what perspective a person speaks from. It frightened me to think of how much power a counselor has over a care seeker; a person seeking direction becomes completely vulnerable, laying their complete trust in your guidance; the person could be easily manipulated. If a counselor isn't properly trained or continually tells the care seeker what to do or just has bad motives, the care seeker could be seriously damaged. Was I ready for such a responsibility?

╬

After celebrating Mass, Richard called me. "Hi, Janet? Do you have some time to talk?"

"Sure. Is something wrong?"

"Well, I just need to talk."

When I arrived at his house, we went for a drive around the neighborhood.

"I spoke to a parishioner earlier today. The last time I talked to her was maybe a month ago. She came up to me and said, 'Thank you, thank you for your help Fr. Richard! I left my husband and now I'm pregnant,' and she was rubbing her stomach. I did not tell her to leave her husband! And I didn't tell her to get pregnant! I never told her that! Then her daughter came up to me later and yelled at me for telling her Mom to go get pregnant by another man. I don't understand. I try to give people instruction and they don't understand. They do the complete opposite!" Richard rubbed his forehead and sighed. With a heaviness in his voice, he began to tell me about the other mishaps he had held in all week. Never until then was I more convinced that a priest's job was something I didn't envy.

"It's hard. I couldn't really tell anybody. But, you, Janet, I could tell you. Thank you, Janet. You know, you are my spiritual director," he said, smiling proudly.

"Hey, you're my spiritual director, too. You've listened to me plenty of times," I said, as we parted.

I was flattered. Truly, I hadn't said that much that evening. I mostly listened. I suppose that was all he needed.

It saddened me that he had few people to talk to. Here he was, someone who had dedicated his entire life to listening to the troubles of parishioners and giving them guidance, and he barely had anyone to turn to. How many other ministers were out there without anyone to confide in?

Thinking of Gloria's class, I thought, maybe I could provide pastoral counseling for clerics, the religious, and lay ministers. But who was I to think I could offer counseling to ministers? Was I some spiritual guru with "powers" to give guidance to priests and nuns? No. But I was a person who somehow had the patience to listen to the troubles of others. Perhaps, it came from losing my parents and clinging to intermittent resurrections that gave me hope. Maybe it was all the love friends and strangers had shown me. Perhaps, I had learned what *not* to do through experiencing the insensitivity of relatives. Crushed hearts eventually grow fervent. Whatever it was, my calling in life seemed to be getting clearer.

Friendships with Diego and the UCLA students left an indelible imprint on me. I felt it my duty to remember what I'd been taught. Being at an institution where a handful of professors understood the importance of culture gave me the confidence that I'd learn more about maintaining one's cultural identity. I wanted to understand the impact of European colonization and United States imperialism on countries that are today considered "developing" or "Third World" countries, and learn about Christianity's role in assimilating and obliterating masses of civilizations. I wanted to remain connected to all my sisters and brothers of color, knowing I was preparing myself not only to serve my Catholic family, but also the family that taught me to nurture my cultural heritage.

Fr. Elias Farajaje-Jones (now known as Ibrahim Farajaje since his conversion to Islam) was among the professors I turned to for this guidance. Whether he stood before the class lecturing or sat down with his students during a circle discussion, his passion and command of the subject matter was incredible. Ibrahim's wealth of knowledge and experience challenging social divides carried wisdom and courage. Ibrahim knew Hebrew, Greek, Aramaic, Latin, German, French, Spanish, Portuguese, Italian, Russian, Old Slavonic, and Arabic. As an esteemed scholar, he also stayed in touch with pop culture, loving songs by Faith Evans and the Black Eyed Peas. Ibrahim was an Eastern Orthodox priest, a bisexual and multiracial (African-American, Native-American, and Irish) man, a father, and a husband.

As Ibrahim, stood before us during his *Interrupting Conversations: Race-ing The(a)ologies* course, he began his lecture on the premium placed on racial purity, "In the late 17th century, the colonization of the Americas, the colonization of Native-Americans, the slavery of Africans, all pervaded the thought of Locke, Hume, and Blumenbach. In 1734 at the University of Göttingen, there was an academy of human racial classification. The teachings were started by Blumenbach who taught a racial hierarchy—one that put 'Caucasians' at the top of the hierarchy…and by the end of the 18th century, progress was the dominant paradigm. There was the idea that race changed form as it passed through different ages; however there remained an immutable essence…If there was a mixing of races, the essence could not be fully communicated. Therefore, racial mixing was disastrous. To be creative, one must be pure."

As I wrote every word into my notebook, I thought of the many times I heard those names touted as great contributors to the Enlightenment. With every lesson, he deconstructed the recording of history, exposing lies that had been passed down as truth; he taught us about the demonization of Blackness and African religions, the persecution of the lesbian, gay, bisexual, transgendered, and questioning community (L.G.B.T.Q.), the importance of maintaining agency as people of color, and the construction of whiteness and white privilege.

Through his courses, my mind was gradually reshaped. In our readers, we had texts from *The Colonizer and the Colonized* by Albert Memmi, *White* by Richard Dyer, *Killing the Black Body* by Dorothy Roberts, *White on Black: Images of Africa and Blacks in Western Popular Culture* by Jan Nederveen Pieterse, and *The Philippines Reader* edited by Daniel Schrimer and Stephen Shalom. Each reading assignment forced me to question everything that I was taught and (not taught) in history and catechism classes since childhood, giving me more facts to support what I had learned at UCLA. And when I had the urge to cross-reference and verify the assertions Ibrahim or these texts made, I asked myself why I questioned these texts when I never questioned, researched, or attempted to verify ideas posited in more mainstream texts.

From Ibrahim, I also learned to recognize myself as a biracial woman—someone who could embrace both sides of my heritage while also understanding the ways I, having light skin, benefit from the misconceptions people have about light-skinned Black people. Conversations with him, attending mixed race conferences, and reading articles Ibrahim recommended, like *Interstitial Integrity* by Rita Nakashima Brock, taught me that being biracial didn't mean I had to view myself as a racially fragmented person condemned to a lifetime of confusion. Throughout my entire life, I tended to switch on and off my two cultures. Depending on whose company I was in, I turned into a chameleon, blending in as best I could. Sometimes, in blatant and subtle ways, I was asked to choose, hearing questions like, "Are you more Black than Filipino or more Filipino than Black?" By such questions, it seemed some people were attempting to determine my authenticity or use my response to justify how "nice" of a Black person I was. As people spent hours staring at me trying to figure me out, asking, "What are you?" I learned quickly how uncomfortable people become if they could not place me in one racial category. Noticing Ibrahim embrace every aspect of himself, I gradually understood that it was okay to embrace both sides and be Black *and* Filipino all the time, creating my own fluid, multidimensional state of being. Beginning to reject my compartmentalized lifestyle and become whole helped me draw from the well of that unique space between cultures.

EXHAUSTION OF BEAUTY

I became entangled with places I vowed never to revisit.

Too many doubles existed within my head without my
knowing.

I am split in two daily
Into days leaving the dawn
        To meet the evening.
And I am left
        At once…bereft.

Right past my present I walk into my former self
        searching.
I begin again
        walking toward my present.
I sink beneath myself where the scent of candle wax
meets urn,
        Turn around to a time when I would struggle to define
and
        Refine myself,
                Only to find myself lost—

A recluse crawls with outstretched hand and raw knees
Through white and bleached inconsistencies
A memory imbibed with the stench of pulsing membranes
        and callous bodies

Gray circles beneath her eyes testify before fellow hearts
        that tried too hard,
Vestiges of collapsed desire.

Listen and listen, for her body is a crucible for rage,
        and love, vision, and fear
And love, bitter, and ache and
        sweetness
Melting in the heat

        misinformed conscience waiting for the proper moment
To revive herself.

Don't tell her this is where hope resides
        because she may discover her strength.
For she may rise with a rage
        frightening venom into a stupor

Claiming her space
        with one step,
causing a room to expand.

She, yes she, no she, will show them goodness.
Misery no longer.
Beauty emerges sending clouds into confusion
        Wondering why she didn't rise sooner.

25

I never got over Diego. It had been two years since I visited him in Boston; and everyday since then, I dreamt he'd change his mind and ask me to be his girlfriend.

Then he emailed me: he was getting married. Her name was Celia. The wedding would be in Phoenix on February 28, 1998, and he wanted me to be there.

I didn't know what to say at first. I silently hoped he would discover this was all a mistake and propose to me. But, it was no mistake.

After tossing and turning many nights, thinking about whether or not I should go, I finally decided it would be best if I went. I wanted to show my support to Diego and his fiancée. Besides, I needed some closure; this could be the perfect kick in the ass to help me get over this man.

I took my last $158 and bought a ticket to Phoenix. With my credit card, I reserved a room at a Motel 6 and rented a car for three days. I was determined to make this trip a retreat—a weekend of transformation.

The Monday before the wedding, he emailed me, asking if there was anything I needed. Six days before the wedding, amidst the insanity of the preparations, he took time to email *me* to see if there was anything *I* needed?! My God! Getting over this beautiful man was going to be the death of me!

Once I landed in Phoenix, I took a shuttle from the airport to Thrifty Rent-A-Car and rented a bright red Geostorm. I drove to Motel 6, dropped off my belongings, and got dinner. When I returned to my motel room, I turned on the television and began wrapping their wedding gift.

From a white box, I pulled out the gift, unwrapping the tissue paper, looking at it, wondering if they would like it. It was an obsidian candleholder made in Oaxaca: when a candle is lit and placed inside the holder, the flame's light flickers through the shapes carved out of the holder so an image of the cosmos is cast around the room. It would create the perfect ambience for a newlywed couple, and at the same time have a cultural significance for both of them.

Instead of buying some generic wedding card, I decided to make my own. Weaving strings of pearls in and out of white card stock, I told myself that if I truly loved Diego, I needed to honor and respect the love he had for Celia, and let him go. To internalize this, each detail became a meditative act: sticking a pearl-headed straight pin through the hole at the top of the crucifix, then through the card, bending the pin in the back; pasting a metallic gold heart on the inside cover, hiding the sharp end of the pin; placing more gold hearts on the inside of the card and covering it with a thin sheet of soft blue tissue paper with roses scattered throughout. The slight shimmer of the gold peeked from behind the tissue paper.

Inside the card, I explained what significance I found in the candle and then wrote:

> ...I pray that you may be watched by all of
> our ancestors, and that they may guide and
> bless your relationship and bless your
> children and their children to come. I pray
> that our children will be able to know each
> other so that they can one day play with
> one another...

I placed the card at the top of the tissue paper that wrapped the candleholder. With pearly white and pink paper, I wrapped the box carefully and placed the finished product on the nightstand.

Getting prepared for the wedding turned into another ritual—a ceremony for myself. Officially, I was letting go and marking this transition with each step I took to get ready.

I woke up early to take a shower; sprayed honeysuckle mist on my body and combed my hair; rubbed honeysuckle lotion on my face and hands; stroked deep burgundy lipstick across my lips; massaged lotion on my legs and squeezed into my black nylons; pulled on my slip and put on my skirt with the light brown leaves and pink and peach flowers. Looking in the mirror, I buttoned my white blouse and finally put on my black blazer, making sure there was plenty of tissue in my pocket. Taking a deep breath and a last look in the mirror, I told myself, "Remain dignified…don't say or do anything dumb." I grabbed the directions and the gift and headed out the door.

I left two hours early just in case I got lost. I drove around 3rd Ave. and Monroe looking for St. Mary's Basilica. I found an old church with the windows boarded up. I pulled over and asked the construction workers nearby, "Do you know where I can find St. Mary's Basilica?" They pointed at the abandoned building, which told me I was lost.

I'll be damned if I came all this way only to miss his wedding, I thought. I drove around in circles for at least twenty minutes before I found another church on 3rd St. and Monroe, four blocks away: St. Mary's Basilica.

When I arrived, I was the first one there. I parked my car in the church parking lot. Taking the opportunity to look around the church, I admired the beautiful architecture and the statue of St. Francis of Assisi. Later, I discovered it was a Franciscan parish.

The pastor came out of the sacristy and said, "Hi, may I help you?"

"I'm just here for a wedding. I'm a little early. Uh, I didn't realize this was a Franciscan parish. I'm a student at the Franciscan School in Berkeley. Would you by chance know Kenan Osborne?"

"Yes, I do," he said, "We went to school together." Small world, I thought.

I returned to my car and waited until I saw other guests arrive. At 11:45 a.m., I stepped out of my bright red car, being quite pleased with my appearance, boosting my ego by telling myself, "Diego, look what you've missed." I walked up the stairs without a teardrop in sight as I entered the church.

And there he was: Diego was standing at the entrance, greeting everyone as they walked in. When he saw me, he immediately gave me a hug. "Oh my God! You made it. Did you get my emails? I needed to know if you were coming and if you needed anything. Well, actually I didn't *need* to know."

"Yeah, I got it. Everything's fine. I'm staying at a Motel 6 downtown," I said, smiling, "Are you nervous?"

"No. I'm ready to go!" he said with excitement.

He introduced me to his friends near the door. Then he introduced me to his parents, and I was completely enamored by their presence, thinking about how they were responsible for raising this beautiful man.

I was escorted down the aisle and his brother handed me a scroll as I sat down.

The ceremony was about to begin. All eyes faced the back of the church. As his mother and Celia's mother walked him down the aisle, Diego looked handsome and confident in his tuxedo.

The wedding march began. And then came Celia—absolutely gorgeous. With her beautiful long black curly hair lightly brushing the detailed embroidery around her cleavage, Celia glowed as she walked down the aisle arm-in-arm with her father and Diego's father.

It was a simple and beautiful ceremony. Violin music. Readings from scripture. Diego and Celia kneeling. The exchange of vows. Diego kissing the bride. And more violins. The priest never said the line: "If there is anyone who objects to this union, let them speak now or forever hold their peace." Thank God I was spared the opportunity to hysterically throw my body across the altar in protest.

I was quite proud of myself, actually; I was watching the love of my life marry the love of his life, and I didn't cry once during the ceremony. Lord knows, I wanted to cry, but my composure was far more important. Preserving my self-dignity was the first priority.

After the ceremony, to test my endurance, I stayed in the church to watch them have their photographs taken. As I sat down in the front row, I looked at them and smiled. Celia smiled and waved at me, which took me by surprise. I waved and smiled back, wondering how she knew who I was. Did Diego point me out to her? Had she seen a picture of me before? I didn't know and it didn't matter. The image of them standing together in each others' arms was engraved in mind and overshadowed those questions; as I became used to the idea of them as a couple, I silently wished them well.

Later, Diego's mom and I found ourselves standing next to each other.

"Diego has mentioned you," she said, "Thank you for being such a good friend to him."

"Oh," I said, not knowing how to respond, "He's been a really good friend to me." Quickly changing the subject, I asked, "Do you know exactly where the reception is?"

"No. I have no idea. I don't know what's happening…I don't know where anything is…It's so much different from when my daughter got married. Before, I knew everything that was happening. I knew where the pots and pans were. I knew where the reception would be. This time, I don't know anything…"

Though I felt like I was getting too much information, I was flattered that she was comfortable enough to tell me so much. Unable to resist the temptation, as she spoke, I secretly imagined her as my mother-in-law.

⁜

The air was hot and dry on the way to Mesa, where the reception took place. Yellowish-brown land extended for miles on both sides of the road. Cactus trees and tumbleweeds were sprinkled every few feet across the desert. When I arrived, people were still setting up, and I was, once again, the first one there. I left my gift on the gift table, being proud it was the first, and went for a drive, breathing in more heat, becoming increasingly anxious to talk to Celia.

When I returned, the reception was beginning to fill up. Inside, the seating was prearranged with labels at each place setting. I was seated with Celia's friends, who one by one introduced themselves to me. All of them met her at Stanford as undergraduates. I was the only one at the table who was a friend of Diego's, which made me feel slightly awkward. Nonetheless, they helped me feel comfortable, always including me in their conversations, when they, given their history together, could have socialized without me.

Diego and Celia walked from table to table, greeting their guests. As I watched them, I wanted to be happy, and not place my air of dignity in jeopardy, but my sadness hit me like a blow to the stomach, causing a sullen daze to come over my face and my whole body to be numb. Not realizing how transparent I'd become, one of Celia's friends leaned toward me and said, "A little cake might cheer you up!" Somebody noticed. Damn!

Diego and Celia prepared for their first dance. To redeem myself and prove to any suspicious eyes that I was happy for the newlyweds, I left my seat and stood a few feet from the couple to take a picture. When I looked through the camera, I discovered that I wasn't proving anything; I just needed the reality check, again.

It was after dark, and the DJ started playing some R&B and Hip Hop. Immediately, Celia's friends took to the dance floor and invited me to join them. Dancing kept my mind off my sadness. When the timing was right, I took the chance to speak to Celia, partly to avoid Diego and partly as a gesture to Celia that I had no intention of getting with her man.

"Congratulations," I said, smiling.

"Oh, thank you," said Celia. Then somehow, at the height of my eagerness to avoid a silent gap, we arrived at the topic of body piercing.

"Yeah, I used to have a nose ring. A little rhinestone, right here," I pointed, "But then a pimple grew under it and I had to take it out. And then the hole closed up."

"Oh really? My cousin had her tongue pierced," she said, as I winced. We went on and on about the joys and pains of piercings and other random topics. By the end of the conversation, I was disappointed to find no flaws in her. Celia was gorgeous. She had a great figure. She was genuine. She could dance. She was poised. And…she was a lawyer—a graduate of Harvard Law School. The woman was beautiful, intelligent, and classy. I couldn't find a damn thing wrong with her!

The dancing continued, and I decided to leave early to not prolong the agony and to keep from saying or doing something stupid. I approached Diego's parents. "It was a real pleasure meeting both of you," I said, holding their hands.

I walked over to Celia who was huddled around the fireplace with her friends. Getting eye contact with her, I said, "Celia, I'm going to go now. I just wanted to tell you congratulations," giving her a hug, "It was so nice meeting you."

And finally, I went to Diego. He was standing next to his parents, when I held both of his hands and said, "Diego, she's just as beautiful as you described her. I wish you two my very best." There was no better match for Diego.

"Thank you," he said with a gentle smile.

I slowly released his hands, turned my back, and walked out the door as if into a distant sunset. I exhaled, relieved that I hadn't made a fool of myself. My dignity was fully intact. The initial step of gaining closure was over. The rest had to be done alone.

"I can't believe he emailed me a week before the wedding," I said to Richard, explaining the whole story as we both walked up the stairs of his house, "and then he hugged me when I came into the church and introduced me to all his friends and his parents. His mom even said that

Diego had told her about me! I don't understand. Was I that important to him? How close were we?"

"Yeah, you cannot drink the water and forget the glass," Richard said plainly. I began to cry. I remembered him tell me in Boston, "Your emails give me a good springboard that help me articulate and test out my ideas"; and then I recalled something he wrote after I had "confessed my undying love":

> "…In terms of our friendship, I would be seriously distraught if it couldn't be resuscitated. If I could just be so bold: I think that this society does not teach us how to deal with emotional relationships. All it really trains us to believe is that if we feel some connection to another person, it must be romantic. I think that what we have, for example, is a very intimate spiritual relationship, one that can be emotional and rational and that we can explore in all its depth in that capacity…we simply have no model to work from…so we'll just have to construct it.

No, our relationship was not a romantic one, but it was intimate. It was difficult to believe, but, as his friend, I had given him something, whatever that something was; I did mean something to him.

⌗

Two weeks after the wedding, I opened my mailbox and found a thank you card from Diego and Celia. I opened the card and read:

Dear Janet:

Your gift was so thoughtful, the idea behind the candle really touched both of us. It was so nice having you at the wedding—you not only warmed the reception with your personality, but you represented a very dear community in my life. Thank you so much, and I look forward to hearing from you again soon.

Love,
Diego and Celia

About a month passed before I responded:

Hi Diego:

I received your card. Thank you very much. You know, I had an absolutely wonderful time at your wedding and I am so grateful that Celia's friends took me under their wing. It was great. Anyways, since you're my friend, I think I owe you an explanation as to why I have not written to you since your wedding. I'll keep it short and simple. I was trying to "give you up" for the Lenten season. It was my little way of letting go. I have to admit that I miss the conversations we used to have over email. You have literally changed my life in tremendous ways. It's interesting because I am now in dialogue with a couple of Biblical studies graduate students here at the G.T.U. (neither of whom are Christian; both of whom are staunchly against missionary work) and a philosophy doctorate student from U.C.I. These are conversations that I would have never engaged in three years ago. I have not used these to replace my conversations with you, but perhaps as a means of going forward.

Anyways, I do not feel comfortable writing to you in the same amount of detail as before. I think that it would be a severe disrespect to Celia if I did. Any correspondence I do send to you, I intend to address to both you and Celia...I think this would be most appropriate.

Well, how can I be a friend to you? How can I be a friend to Celia? Be completely honest.

In Christ,
Janet

And Diego replied:

Dear Janet:

It's taken me awhile to respond cuz I've been at a loss for what to say. My immediate reaction was confusion. I'd heard something similar from another friend (she said that someone told her that she shouldn't be writing postcards to someone who was married) and I just wasn't getting it (this other friend agreed with me, and will continue writing). There's nothing static about friendships; they're meant to change and adapt w.r.t. changing conditions. But that's just how I would like things to be; it doesn't really account for anyone else's previous experiences or expectations. (Celia calls me out on this all the time: of course things make sense in my little theoretical world, but we're only partially living there.) So I guess my only recourse is to leave it to you. Whatever variety of email correspondence you feel comfortable with will be ok with me, from joint mailings (you, me, and Celia on every addressal) to once-a-year form letters.

I should let you know that I brought this up with Celia, and she leans towards my perspective. The way she explained it to me, she sees all the people I've been in contact with in my life converge into who I am today. To start cutting people out is to change the person she fell in love with—not necessarily a good thing. On the other hand circumstances are kind of taking care of this issue for a little while. June 1st, I'll be heading to Mexico for the summer, and there I'll be cut off from email and—practically speaking—postal mail. If you'd like, we can just leave this whole thing on the backburner until we've both gained the perspective of a few months time.

Saludos,
Diego

In spite of all my self-imposed reality checks, my feelings for Diego were still tender. Even though he and Celia saw no problem with me corresponding with him, I still did. Temporarily staying out of contact seemed like the only way I could completely reimagine my life without him. I didn't want to forget him; there was no way I could. He made an impression on me that was profound: he taught me how to be patient and how to listen; he changed the way I saw other religions; he changed the way I lived my life. No, I didn't want to forget him—just move forward. Circumstances worked in my favor while he was in Mexico. And when he returned, I never wrote back to him.

26

With Richard's help, I planned to do youth ministry in Tanzania during the summer of 1998. However, around May, the funding for the plane ticket never came through. For weeks, I fumbled around trying to apply for summer ministry programs across the country only to encounter the same problem—lack of funds to cover travel expenses.

I panicked. My apartment had already been rented out for the summer. I had no money and no job to support myself during those three months. Finally, I considered my last resort—the Shepardsons. While in Riverside, I asked them for so many favors that I was afraid that by this time, I had already tested their patience.

As I picked up the phone, I was more nervous and more disappointed in myself than ever. Diana, Mr. Shepardson's wife, answered the phone, "Hello?"

"Hi, this is Janet. How are you?"

"Fine. How are you? Any luck finding a summer program?"

"No. Actually, I wanted to ask you…do you think it would be alright if I stayed with you this summer?"

"Yes. Yes, Janet," she said without hesitation, "We can pay for a portion of your train ticket."

"Oh, thank you. Thank you for letting me stay with you," I said, "And I'll pay for the rest of the ticket. When I get down to Lancaster, I'll find a job."

"Okay, Janet, but you don't have to pay rent or pay for groceries. You just save the money for the upcoming school year. I'll call around. There might be someone I know that has a job opening."

I thought about seeing if Sacred Heart Catholic Church, the parish I grew up in, had an opening for a youth ministry position. Just in case, I spent a week before my arrival preparing a six-session youth ministry plan, with activities and publicity strategies, to make myself more marketable. Regardless of how slight the possibility would be, I was confident that I would definitely "wow" the pastor with my enthusiasm and my portfolio. There's nothing I could lose.

╬

"The Lord is good to me and so I thank the Lord. For giving me, the things I need. The sun and the rain and the apple seed. The Lord is good to me. Amen!" The five of us smiled after singing grace my first night at the Shepardsons' home. We sat at the table, ready for dinner: Mr. Shepardson sat at the head of the table, Diana was across from me, Katie, the oldest child, sat next to me, while Anna, the youngest, was in her high chair next to Diana. Plates were passed around and filled with the evening's meal, while Tom explained to the children, "Now Katie, Anna, Janet will be staying with us this summer. She will be a part of our family." They looked at me smiled with excitement. I looked at them and smiled, too.

After dinner, Mr. Shepardson and Diana showed me where I would be staying. "Now here's your room. There are some hangers for your clothes here in the closet and a little bag for your laundry," Diana said as she raised the red and white-checkered laundry bag. I was moved by the thought of them clearing out their spare bedroom and preparing it just for me.

"Have a goodnight honey," Mr. Shepardson said as he hugged me.

"Goodnight, sweetie," Diana said, "Just let us know if you need anything, okay?"

"Okay," I said, hugging her, and then Katie and Anna. "Thank you again."

Even though, at first, I felt awkward and out of place, I was comforted by their generosity. Diana and Mr. Shepardson did everything to help me feel at home. That night I fell asleep in disbelief of how kind they were.

The following morning, I immediately began job hunting. Phone call, after phone call was made, until within minutes, I reached Fr. O'Farrell, the pastor of Sacred Heart, who invited me for an interview later that week.

Not knowing what to expect, I walked into his office with my portfolio, and made my proposal, "Hi, I'm Janet Stickmon. Thanks for setting up the interview," I said with confidence. "Well, I'm a graduate student at the Franciscan School of Theology in Berkeley. I'm interested in offering some workshops to your youth ministry. I have a portfolio including the description of each of the workshops," I said, handing it to him.

He adjusted his bifocals and perused through each page. "Quite impressive. Quite impressive. Very nice. However, I'm afraid that there's no position available for youth ministry. We just found a new youth minister. But, you know, there is a secretarial position available if you're interested. Possibly, you can assist the newly assigned youth minister on the side. We'll pay you for that on an hourly basis."

"Yes, that would be great," I said, pleased with how painless the interview was.

"Okay, can you start in two days, on Thursday?"

"Yes, that sound's good. I'll be here."

"Guess what?" I said to the Sheps, standing in the kitchen, "I found a job! I'll be the receptionist in the rectory at Sacred Heart Church. The pastor said I can help the youth minister on the side! I can't believe it!"

"Already? You just got here!" Diana said smiling, as Mr. Shepardson smiled, too.

"Well, Janet," Mr. Shepardson began, pausing for a moment, "you have a certain inner divine spark about you that people recognize when they see it," he said, seemingly unsurprised by the news.

"Janet, we can teach you how to drive a stick so you can borrow the white car this summer," Diana said with excitement.

I couldn't believe how quickly and easily things were happening. Within days, everything fell right into place.

⚟

Every morning, for the first two weeks, Mr. Shepardson dropped me off at a coffee shop near work before he left to teach summer school. During these rides to work, I learned much about him that was never obvious to me when I was in high school.

Mr. Shepardson (or Tom as I later called him once he convinced me it was alright) was patient and modest—an intelligent man with an understated sense of humor that won the hearts of high school students and adults alike. Being fairly reserved, he was very thorough, carefully choosing his words. He described himself as "an introvert with extrovert skills that developed out of necessity."

Since we shared this in common, in addition to many other things, he noticed certain qualities of mine that

I'd always considered quirky. For instance, on the way to work one morning, while I was putting on lipstick, Tom said, "You look nice today."

"Thank you," I said softly, slightly embarrassed.

"Do you have difficulty accepting compliments?" he asked.

"Uh, yeah," I said, shifty-eyed, feeling like an amateur magician whose secrets had been exposed.

"Yes, I know, partly because I know you well and also because I know myself very well. We're very much alike."

Knowing someone else who was uncomfortable with compliments and was just as much an introvert as I, seemed to validate my existence. For most of my life, I was somewhat self-conscious and preferred not drawing unnecessary attention to myself. I had always been aware of how reticent and awkward I could be around new faces, sometimes finding myself stuttering or fidgeting. The more genuine and trustworthy a person seemed, the more comfortable and the less inhibited I became. This gradually changed during my undergraduate years, but as an adult I felt the remnants of this awkwardness pop up every now and then.

However, watching Tom's comfort with his personality made me less insecure. In his presence, I was my complete self and felt comfortable being quiet without explaining or apologizing. The last time I felt acceptance like this was with my own parents.

╬

After getting a taste of the energy in the Bay Area, being back in Lancaster was a step backward. Downtown was lifeless. And the coffee shop where I waited every morning was only a place where people could grab a quick bite to eat, not a place where they could relax and read a novel or write in their journals or have meaningful conversations. Staring at the traffic through the coffee shop window—one car every twenty minutes—I tried counting my blessings: I have a job, a loving family to live with, and I don't have to pay rent. Finishing my last sip of apple juice, I threw the carton away and walked up the street to Sacred Heart, counting my blessings again.

I unlocked the rectory door and sat at my desk. As the receptionist, I answered the door, took phone messages, set appointments for the priests, and prepared baptismal, wedding, and funeral records.

The rectory was a spiritual emergency room. Every person who came through the front door had some dire emergency: a person wants to meet with a priest for counseling; another, out of breath, needs baptismal records immediately since she's getting married in Mexico in a month; a few starving regulars come for dry Cup-O-Noodles; a homeless man comes looking for toenail clippers; a young man threatens to commit suicide if he doesn't speak to a priest that minute. There were times I didn't want to answer the door, fearing the drama that was waiting for me. And by 5 p.m., I encountered every combination of circumstances imaginable. Exhausted, I said goodbye to the other staff members and locked the door, convinced that rectories were the single reason Catholic churches still exist.

After work, Diana and Tom took turns bringing me to the parking lot at Quartz Hill High School to practice driving. As I jerked and stalled, I silently recited what each of them taught me: get in first gear, step on the clutch, step on gas, ease off clutch, drive, brake slowly, don't ride the clutch, ease on to it, the clutch should be all the way down by the time you stop. And again: first gear, clutch, gas, off clutch, brakes, clutch, gas, off clutch. Oh, shit!! Start the car, clutch, first gear, clutch…

When I advanced to actually driving on streets, Tom said, "When you step on the clutch think of it opening up, allowing the gears to move. Oh, and sometimes it can be difficult to make sure the car is in first, so just think of somebody you hate, and hit it to the left and push it up." Picturing Rovalia, I found myself in first gear without a problem.

If they ever became impatient with me, I couldn't tell. When I stalled, Tom and Diana calmly told me to start again, never raising their voices. I felt like that 15-year old child that drove Mom's '78 Ford Fairmont once around the parking lot of the Antelope Valley Fairgrounds, only months before she died. Tom and Diana were seeing me through a rite of passage that was never completed.

╬

Diana and I spent a lot of time together in the park, on the front lawn, and in the kitchen preparing dinner. The first time I ever saw her was at Back to School Night at Antelope Valley High School when I was 14 years old. I could remember her beauty and her effortless, radiant smile. Ten years later, I still recognized that smile and discovered that her character was just as beautiful as her appearance.

Diana was most definitely an extrovert—a very animated woman with an energy that was exciting and contagious. When Tom spoke of her, he often said, "If we were both like me, we'd fall asleep."

The woman's openness to me was amazing. What experiences Tom shared with his students, seemed to also be shared by Diana. This could only explain why her warmth and welcoming spirit could be extended to me, a person she had little personal contact with until that summer.

I felt a sisterly kinship with her. Our exchanges ranged from passionate debates about homosexuality to intimate discussions about Diego. Her intuition and thoughtfulness gave her the ability to anticipate my needs in a way that no one in my family ever did: everything from surprising me with my favorite candy bar to saying the perfect words to ease my conscience. Once, after telling her the Rovalia story and how I was accused of taking advantage of the family's hospitality, she said, "But, Janet. You're a giver. You've always been a giver." I didn't know what to say. After years of blaming myself for not being accepted by family, I was comforted that someone actually noticed the ways I have tried to give.

Diana made many observations about my life that forced me to realize that I believed lies about myself; some of these were lies fed to me by others and some were lies of my own design created for survival. She once told me, "Janet, you'd never know that you'd experienced the things you have because you are so normal." Indeed, I had made great efforts to appear "normal" to avoid inviting the sort of pity that mentioning my "imperfect" family background usually inspired. At the same time, there was a cost: I never accepted myself for not being "normal"—for not having the perfect background. The normalcy I chased was a fantasy.

I didn't know how much I hated myself until Diana stopped to look at me during one of our conversations in the kitchen and asked, "Do you know how special you are?"

I stood, looking at her, silent. Being told I was worth something was foreign to me. "I wasn't a burden? She actually likes having me around?" I thought to myself.

There was a time when I once believed I was special, but somehow that got lost.

⚓

One night, when I was already in bed, I heard a knock on the bedroom door.

"Yes," I said.

The door cracked open. "I just wanted to tell you goodnight," Tom said.

I got up, gave him a hug. "Goodnight," I said.

"Goodnight, honey," he said, closing the door. It had been a long time since anyone said goodnight to me. Upon realizing that, I cried, wiping my tears on my pillow. Had he never said goodnight to me, I doubt I would have noticed how long it had been since I'd received the slightest bit of affection.

Another time, I woke up in the middle of the night with a headache. Half asleep, I walked to the kitchen to look for aspirin in the cupboard. Tom was sitting on the couch reading a book. "Hi," I said, "I'm gonna get some Tylenol. I have a headache."

"Okay," he said, looking concerned. I fumbled around a little bit, bumping cans and cups together. Tom quietly walked to the cupboard, reached for the aspirin bottle, opened it, and handed me a couple pills. He poured me a glass of water and handed it to me. I swallowed the aspirin. "Thank you," I said, and returned to bed.

"You're welcome. Goodnight honey," he said as he returned to the couch to read.

His gentleness reminded me I was fatherless—that I was parentless. Over the years, I had become so callous in order to prevent myself from being hurt—numb to all emotions so I couldn't feel pain or break down in self-pity. In doing so, I also cut myself off from feeling genuine joy. I taught myself to get used to being alone so I could survive without relying on anyone's help or affection. And I was very successful. Very safe. My self-made armor was impenetrable to everyone—well, almost everyone.

╬

Near the end of July, Tom drove me to the home of my mother's friend so I could spend time with her. On the way, he asked me, "So how did you become so interested in culture," knowing I had taken an interest in cultural identity.

"It started with the McNair Star program and then summer research programs that reached out to students of color. Really it started with UCLA. There were so many students there who were very aware of their ethnic backgrounds. Being in Lancaster, I learned to hate myself. You know, I never believed I was attractive because I was Black," I said.

"Was this a result of things people had said to you?" he asked.

"It was a combination of a few explicit things said and an overwhelming number of implicit messages, particularly living in a predominantly white environment."

"But in my class, you seemed like a really positive individual," he said, confused, "You didn't seemed to be filled with hate."

"Yeah, I was pretty positive then and even after Mom's death," I said, remembering how I proudly told him in high school, "All Filipinos stick together!" confident that one of my relatives would take care of me. "I didn't think I could draw confidence from my appearance so I drew confidence from other things like my intellect or my achievements in art, track, and band. This seemed like enough to sustain me. I'm a little surprised when men tell me I'm pretty. It's hard to accept when all your life you've believed that you were unattractive."

"Diana and I have always admired your beauty, not just because you were beautiful but because it was also a reflection of your cultural heritage," he said.

"Oh, I hated the way I looked growing up," I said, covering my face, weeping.

Later, as we pulled up to the house and waited until Mom's friend arrived, we spoke more about what it meant to live in a predominantly white environment. "It was hard because I didn't have any role models. I only had one Black teacher during my entire education before college. Since I didn't have any role models, I just became my own."

"I like that…you became your own role model," he said, pondering the idea. "I am disappointed that I can't be a role model to my Black students," he said, "With the Black students I have, I'm afraid to give them too much attention in fear that they will think I'm doing so because they are Black."

"I think you can still be a role model to a certain degree—to the degree that you are willing to speak against the injustice of racism in a classroom that is a white majority and also do so among your white colleagues…to the degree that you give agency to people of color, not being ready to explain to them what their culture is but to allow them to speak for themselves…" I said.

Mom's friend hadn't arrived yet, so we decided to swing by her restaurant to see if she was there. On the way, the conversation shifted. I wanted to tell him how much I missed him the previous weekend when he was away, but was unsure where to begin.

"I missed you," I said.

"I missed you, too," he responded politely.

"You know, my friend and I…we were talking and I told her that…well, when I get married I want you to walk me down the aisle." He looked at me intently and held my hand. I held his arm with both hands like little girl clinging to her father, crying, "You've been a daddy to me. You help me feel beautiful." I had never felt more special than when I was with him. Since Mom died, I only thought about what was missing from my life since I had no mother. I never wondered what effect having no father had on me. Though Tom didn't replace Da'y, he was a person who had known me since I was a teenager and therefore had the ability to remind me of the gifts that I forgot I possessed.

⚌

The Shepardsons and I spent our last night together at a baseball game. I was no big fan of baseball, but being with them was enough. After the game, we walked to the bottom of the stands and approached the parking lot. "Wait," I said, "Let's take a picture together." I found a stranger willing to take a picture of us, as we posed: Tom, Diana, Katie, and Anna surrounding me in the center.

It was warm that night as the five of us walked to the parking lot. The summer was over. I didn't want to leave them. Diana placed Anna in the car seat, and then walked behind the car where I stood; Katie was at her side. Diana's eyes began to well up with tears. Katie hugged me so tightly and began to cry, as well. Hearing her mom and sister crying, Anna, joined in, too. Diana looked at Anna and smiled. She hugged me, then taking my face in her hands, she said, "Even though we may not always agree, know that we always support you." Crying, she shook me and asked, "Do you realize how special you are? Do you?" I began to cry and only looked at her. I hugged Diana again, then Katie. "Thank you for everything you've given me. Thank you," I said, still looking at Diana before walking to the other car where Tom was waiting.

I wanted to say goodbye to my mother's friend before leaving Lancaster, so Tom agreed to drop me off at her house. Few words were exchanged during the ride. And when we arrived, he walked me to the door of her home and gave me a warm hug. "Follow your dreams," he said simply. I watched as he walked slowly to the white car and backed out of the driveway to return home. I walked away knowing I wasn't just *like* a part of their family—I *was* family.

27

During the ride home, I sat on the train, looking out the window at the ocean, finding it strange to be alone again. I had become used to having a family, even if it was only for three months. Being alone made it difficult to believe that in ten years I had grown accustomed to being isolated. I had lived on survival mode since Mom died without realizing how much love was missing from my life. The Shepardsons filled a void I didn't know I had. And since then, I wondered how I ever lived without a family's love in the first place.

When I arrived in Berkeley, I drug my luggage about five blocks to the nearest pay phone to call a cab. Sitting on a cold concrete bench near a grocery store parking lot, I counted the minutes, looking around to pass the time: homeless people shuffled by; mothers holding grocery lists and children walked in the store and out with bags of groceries. Waiting for a stranger to pick me up, not a friend or relative, only intensified my loneliness. A half-hour passed before a yellow cab pulled into the parking lot.

Once I was home, I walked up the stairs, hearing them creak with each step. The floor shook as I walked down the hall. And then I entered my apartment: cold stale air hit my face; my old, raggedy couch still there; the walls, empty; a layer of dust collected on my broken coffee table; boxes of kitchen utensils were tucked away in the cupboards. I sat on the couch in my livingroom/bedroom/familyroom, looking around for awhile, realizing I was miserable without my new family.

I went downstairs to Tim's apartment, even though I didn't know him very well. "Hi, um, do you have a little time to chat?" I asked.

"Sure, come on in," he said.

"I just got back from staying with this family all summer. And, uh, I just didn't feel like being alone."

"Really? How was it?"

"Oh God, it was so nice. I stayed with my high school history teacher and his family. They didn't treat me like some outsider; they treated me like family," I began, telling him about the summer from beginning to end. He nodded and smiled, looking interested.

When I finished, I asked him, "So how was your summer?"

"Well, not so good. My fiancée broke off our engagement. I just don't understand. We had already planned the whole ceremony with Fr. Richard and she just broke it off," he said in disbelief.

"I'm so sorry," I said, pausing for a moment. "So what happened? Did she tell you why?"

"No! She just came here and told me she didn't want to get married. She didn't say why. I'm so pissed! I mean…maybe I wouldn't be so mad, if I actually knew why, but I don't," he said, exasperated.

"God, that doesn't make any sense. You would think she'd at least give you a reason."

"Yeah, I know," he said, looking down at the floor.

We sat in his kitchen in silence for a few minutes. I suppose Tim and I were meant to keep each other company that afternoon.

When I returned to my apartment, I tried making sense out of the summer. Was God trying to show me how it felt to be with a family that really cared? Was God telling me to forget my blood relatives and redefine what family is?

Was God giving me a glimpse of what family could be so I could try to establish the same closeness with my own relatives?

Later that week, I walked to a coffee shop to reflect on the summer. Pulling out a sheet of scratch paper from my backpack, I began writing. It was no ordinary journal entry, though. Scattered feelings and snapshots of moments with Tom and Diana were emptied onto the page. Twenty minutes later, I immediately stuffed the paper into my backpack and walked home, feeling inspired to write a poem. After three hours of erasing and replacing lines and stanzas and trying to choose the right words, it was finished. I called it "Did You Know?"

The following morning, I emailed the poem to a couple of friends at F.S.T. and it was met with a great response. They recommended I read it at an open mic, but I was hesitant; the poem wasn't intended to read publicly; it was only meant to help me get some feelings out on paper.

However, as the weeks passed, more themes for poems flooded my head: invisibility, resurrection, redefining self. Images rushed to mind, and I quickly jotted down notes on napkins and scratch paper and receipts, trying to keep up with them and hoping that eventually they'd find their way into poems. The images and words had a pulse, a rhythm, a shade telling me I had no control over my source of inspiration. This latent voice controlled me and couldn't wait to unravel its string of emotions and thoughts so it could be heard.

╫

After the incessant prodding of friends, I read "Did You Know?" at the semifinals for the International Black Writers and Artists Poetry Slam at La Peña Cultural Art

Center. I made it to the finals, having one week to prepare. Even though I didn't like the idea of a poetry competition, I felt the need to prove to myself I could perform it publicly. Pacing around the livingroom, walking to class, returning from the grocery store, I rehearsed that single poem until it was memorized.

On November 22, 1998, the day of the slam, I panicked, worrying that I might stutter or forget a line onstage. All day, I rehearsed the poem again and again, taking deep breaths attempting to calm myself until evening came.

La Peña was packed with beautiful Black faces of every hue reminding me of my first N.S.B.E. conference. The lights were dimmed and round tables with candles were set up around the room. My friends and I found a seat, anxious to hear the other poets. The excitement of the crowd grew as the slam began, while I grew nervous, feeling like a child again, ready to begin my rollerskating routine at a competition. Poet after poet took to the stage until I heard the host say, "And our next poet for the evening is Janet Stickmon." The crowd applauded. My friends went wild.

As I walked onstage, I held a binder with my poem inside and placed it on the music stand just in case I'd forget a line. The stage lights blinded me, and I couldn't see a single face in the audience. I only heard the soft rustle diminish into silence, telling me to begin:

> I lay my hand across your back. You stiffen.
> I hold your face in my hands. You flinch.
> Does the obstinance of disbelief cripple you?
> This life you live, is it so accustomed to instability
> Fear prevents it from knowing the solace of simplicity,
> of affection, of stability?

No. I do not speak of romance.
I speak of contemplation upon the real.

Has your beauty ever held someone's eyes with an
unrelenting embrace,
Sending tears of ambiguity down their face
Crying desperately for more, crying desperately for
mercy?

Are bodies immobilized,
As if Wisdom has stepped before them?
That unforeseen emanation, capable of moving all,
Does it cause bodies to halt before making their
advance?
Perhaps, it has
And you never noticed.

Your scent, your eyes, your thoughts,
Your rich blackness, your Cebuano blood,
Do they intoxicate the proud and the unaware,
Making them soulmates with God?
Perhaps, they have
And you never noticed.

Did they not tell you? Or did you not believe?
Oh, soul of beauty, that fine line separating polite
acceptance of adoration
From internalized love of self has confused and killed
many.
Forsaken compliments, once proudly offered, now lay to
the ground,
Unscathed, but unwanted.

Those vacant spaces of your life, did your lovers fail to
enter them?
Hands never held. Faces never touched. Thoughts
never heard.

Yes, these chasms. Did they know they were filled with blood?
No, they did not.

You never screamed. You never yelled.
You cried, but only with the four walls of many cold rooms.
Vulnerabilities never disclosed.
You simply lived, bound by pretenses,
Aspiring toward survival.

Did they forget to ask,
"Are you aware of the beauty and the hope that sustains you and those you touch?"
So, did they plan to tell you?
When? Soon or never?
So, do you plan to hear them?
When? Soon or never?

Oh, soul of beauty, do not await the arrival of never.
Never has confused and killed many.

You shall not wait.
You have held my eyes.
You have stopped my body.

Feel my hand across your back.
Hold my hands against your face.
Accept this gift.
Not soon. But now.

Cameras flashed in my face. The audience applauded, and I was relieved it was all over. Walking offstage, my kneecaps trembled. But in time, I felt something new…I didn't feel hesitant like I normally did. I felt as if I had physically carved out a home within myself…as if I didn't have to walk into a space and be afraid that I didn't belong...as if publicly calling out what had been seizing me for so many years was enough to free me. I was becoming confident that I *belonged* anywhere I chose to be.

╬

A woman from the back approached me. "That was a really great poem," she said, "Thank you for sharing it with us."

"Thank you," I replied, surprised she went out of her way tell me that.

During the break, I walked around, giving compliments to other poets. When I returned to my seat, a tall, built, young man came to my table. "I really liked your piece," he said, "Would you like to perform with me and a couple friends at Stanford around January or February?"

"Sure. Do you have a card?"

"Yeah, somewhere," he said, taking all his cards from his wallet and flipping through each one. He dropped a few on the floor. I smiled, knowing he probably didn't have one.

"That's okay. You can just write your name and number on my program," I said, as I handed the green program to him. He quickly wrote his information down and handed it back to me. "Thank you. I'll give you a call this week." As he walked away, I glanced at the program. "Shawn Taylor" it read.

╬

"Hi, this is Janet. I was just calling to find out if a date has been set for the Stanford performance," I said, calling Shawn later that week.

"No, nothing yet. I'm still trying to get a hold of the guy at Stanford who's arranging everything. Hey, I wanted to tell you…about your performance the other night…you had a lot of presence…and you looked as if you had to prove something to yourself."

That night, I did have something to prove—I wanted to prove to myself that I could read this poem in front of a crowd…a public proclamation that I had reclaimed myself and my beauty after years of self-loathing. I wondered how Shawn knew, but didn't ask. "Wow, really?" I said, "Thanks. You really think I had good presence?"

"Yeah. You had a lot of presence up there. I'd been waiting for a female performer like you…you inspired me to write that night…but I don't wanna blow your head up or nothin'…"

"No, no, it's just that I'm surprised. It was my first poem I'd ever written or performed."

"Okay, I just didn't want your head to get big, that's all."

We stayed on the phone for about forty-five minutes. He did most of the talking while I listened, wondering when I'd have a chance to speak. Nonetheless, I was amazed at what I was hearing. The whole time he spoke, I took notes, wanting to remember every word.

Shawn grew up in the projects of Brooklyn, and by the age of 26, had traveled to the Philippines, Thailand, and the United Kingdom. His mother was Jamaican and his father, Puerto Rican. As a child, he once lived in the basement of a building where he was bitten by countless rats. Growing up, he was often beaten up by people in the neighborhood who mistook his intelligence for arrogance. He began writing poetry at 17 and had performed all across the United States and the United Kingdom. In his poetry, he used elements of popular culture to deconstruct pop culture, trying to help people realize that when they worshipped pop icons, they were worshipping illusions. As an artist, Shawn's work was far more than just performances; for him, stage entertainment was cathartic and spiritual.

Sprawled out on the floor, holding the phone, I sat in awe of his passion and insight. As he spoke of his travels to the Philippines and his criticisms of pop culture, I became excited about how much we had in common. I tried envisioning us as a couple, however, since I was usually attracted to the mild-mannered-reserved-patient-listener types, his talkative nature became a red flag that eliminated the possibility. And besides, later hearing about his random beliefs in sex before marriage and how Mr. Spock was the ideal person didn't exactly turn me on.

⚟

At a performance I had in San Francisco, I saw Shawn's name on a flyer for *Soul Searches*, a spoken word show in Oakland. Since I'd never seen him perform, I figured this could be a good opportunity. Within a few days, I called him, "Hi Shawn. Hey, I just saw your name on a flyer for *Soul Searches*. I'd like to see you perform, but, uh, I don't have a ride there. Do you think I could ride with you?"

"Sure."

"How about we meet in front of this coffee shop down on Euclid…Brewed Awakening?"

"Okay, I'll pick you up at about 6:00 p.m."

I waited in front of the coffee shop, leaning against a telephone pole. Shawn pulled up to the curb in his white car. When I stepped in, he said, "You are so beautiful.

Whoever ends up with you will be really lucky. I wish I didn't like someone in theology school. If I kissed you, will I piss spiders or something? I don't want to be cursed or anything because I'm a heathen!" He spoke so fast his words seemed to run together.

I smiled, unable to say anything. Sitting in the passenger seat, a million thoughts ran through my mind, "Wow! He likes me. I can't believe he just blurted it out like that. Piss spiders? Kiss? Does he really believe he'd be cursed? Maybe he's just trying to be funny. Maybe this was a mistake." He continued to talk, while I sat stiff and guarded, knowing I was taking a big risk getting in a car with a man I didn't know too well.

We finally arrived. It was an art gallery. As we walked in, Shawn introduced me to his friends, and I couldn't help but be enamored with the space: dim and intimate; large paintings hung from the walls; candles flickered onstage with flowers laid all around. Young black, brown, yellow faces filled the room, sporting a brazen spectrum of fashion—leather jackets to camouflage, head wraps and sarongs to knit caps and jeans. The soothing mood of the atmosphere coupled with the warm spirit in the room made me feel I'd stepped into an alternate universe connecting all who entered. I felt like I'd found home.

The featured artists performed first. Spoken word and songs were shared with the crowd, revealing their deepest thoughts and feelings as if giving the audience a piece of themselves to take home. Know yourself. Social change. Freedom. Revolution. All of these were common themes throughout the evening. And with each passionate performance, the audience was drawn in closer.

It was Shawn's turn. He walked onto the stage holding a spiral notebook, preparing to read a piece called

"Juggling Mirrors." He told me he had a difficult time writing a piece for this show because it required him to write about himself; he wasn't used to doing that. He was also uncomfortable reading off paper, since he usually memorized his pieces. Despite his reservations, his performance was amazing. His charisma flooded the stage and poured into the crowd. The fervor in his voice was solid and yet, vulnerable. Our attention was fixed on him from the moment he began until the moment he reached his final line, speaking of his desire to just give a woman "a simple, gentle kiss on the forehead." The innocence of that line made me smile; I saw a side of him I never noticed before.

After the features were done, there was an open mic where I performed, "Your Personal Prophet"—another poem inspired by the Shepardsons. When I stood up, my legs trembled and my hands were nearly dripping. But as I began, I became confident, knowing that this crowd would understand every word:

> Oh, Teacher. Prophet. Companion.
> Announce. Foretell. Prepare.
> You clear paths with the stroke of your wrists,
> premonitions in hand.
> Like John and his water of baptism and the sandals he
> will never carry,
> Let your sweet water run through the aches of my wry
> existence,
> Redefining scents, reclaiming pieces of the self.
> Revelation comes to you with the painful ringing in the
> ear like Muhammad.
> Like a mother creating, transforming into visionary,
> revolutionary.
> Oh teacher, will you be my personal prophet?

> *Yes, I will be your personal prophet.*

Assigning new meaning to old memories.
For you, a sweet scent evokes the pains,
the disbelief of horror,
Of aimless wandering,
wandering with hands that hold
unfulfilled hope,
With no conceivable place for planting or blossoming,
Awaiting the untimely arrival of spring's bloom.
Hands that stopped reaching before
reaching became an option.
I'll be your teacher,
The most loving vocation one could ever undertake,
Take, take my hand and I will show you.
Yes, I will be your personal prophet.

You say yes, but do you know what yes means?   All
goodness besieged.
Fragrances of creams grant the average soul a brief
escape.
But for me, there was no escape.
The honeysuckle blossom, reminiscent of clotted blood
and still fear.
For awhile, I thought the flowers lost their fragrance,
Then I realized I lost my sense of smell.
Who is willing to cross the threshold of this inferno,
where deafening echoes are whispered by
unseen lips?

If you dare redefine the scent left behind by fallen rose
petals,
Do you promise to gather the scattered petals, as well?
Will you help me reclaim what I deliberately lost?
Lost in the throes of conformity and the brittle bars of
essentialism
Forcing me to wait in the confines of my freedom.
Black or Pilipina? Pilipina or Black?
More Pinay than Black? More Black than Flip?
You knew these were the wrong questions!!

From my feet stretch the roots to my ancestors of Labangon, and
To my ancestors of Africa...where in Africa, I have no memory...
Reclaiming pieces of a fragmented and rich legacy,
Transcending generations giving birth to my spirit of today.
Urging my arms to reach out to my tomorrow.

Help me retrieve the precious gifts you thought too highly of,
          the gems I thought too little of.
You know, I may not recognize them, but you might.
Because you knew me.

Will you tell me I'm enough today,
Today to set me free,
Free so I may fully become who I already am.
Will you be my personal prophet?

> *Yes, I'll be your personal prophet?*
> *Like the lover sings to the beloved: "I'll try to help you remember."*
> *Not by my power, but yours.*
> *You will gather the forgotten pieces*
>   *buried by false maturity,*
> *Drawing them into the new.*
> *Now able to smell beauty in the creams,*
>   *in the violets.*
> *Able to recognize the sound of pain.*
> *Take, take my hand and you will show me.*

Everyone's eyes were fixed on me. As I performed the piece, I saw nodding heads and smiles and heard random claps dart across the room like falling stars. And when I was finished, the cheers and applause told me they understood.

I returned to my seat, my knees trembling harder than when I first began. Shawn turned to me and gave me a hug. And as we listened to the remaining performers, we sat shoulder to shoulder, my arm resting on him.

When the evening came to an end, the expressions on everyone's faces looked as if they had just been to church. People left feeling healed and exhausted from their emotional and spiritual high.

╬

In the car, Shawn spoke most of the way home. "Why will you only meet me in a public place and not your apartment?" he asked, "I'm not trying to get in your pants or anything."

Again, I was stunned speechless. I was relieved to hear he didn't want to get in my pants, but did he have to be so crude? "Well, I just preferred meeting you in a public place, that's all," I said, not telling him that whenever I had a crush on a guy, I knew him from school or church or a fellowship meeting. There was always one other person who knew the person I was interested in. This time, I didn't have any friends who knew Shawn. The spoken word circle was foreign to me. I assumed anyone I hadn't met through school or church may not be safe; so I stayed cautious.

Shawn got out of the car and walked me to the stairs, holding my hand.

"Are there going to be nuns and priests looking out their windows to see what we're doing?" he asked.

"No," I said, wondering whether or not he was serious. We reached the top of the stairs. When I gave him a hug, he turned his head and kissed me. Some silence passed.

"So what does this mean?" he asked, "Is this real or are you just overwhelmed by the energy of tonight's show?"

"I don't know," I said.

"Can I call you?"

"Yes…on one condition. That you let me do some of the talking."

"Okay," he said, smiling as he went down the stairs.

I walked down the hallway trying to sort out my thoughts. I didn't expect Shawn to kiss me. And I wasn't sure what it meant or if I was interested in dating him. To make matters more complicated, earlier that day I met Ray, a man who slipped me his phone number during a workshop at a mixed race conference. Situations like this never happened to me.

╬

The following day, while Ray and I were on the phone, Shawn called on the other line. In a panic, I bounced back and forth between lines, trying to figure out what to say to each of them, eventually telling Ray I'd call him back.

"Hi, how are you?" Shawn asked.

"Um, fine. How are you?"

"Fine. I just wanted to ask you…what did that kiss mean to you?"

"I don't know. I, um…I think I just want to be friends…I have to be honest with you. I met someone yesterday, before the show…I think I'm going to pursue a relationship with him. I'm sorry," I said, feeling as though I had strung him along.

Shawn couldn't accept my answer. "We had passed the boundaries of friendship," he said, "I had a vision of you at my house. We were in bed together cuddling…we weren't doing anything. We were just cuddling. It was almost premonitory. I let you in. I fell for you. Being in your presence was a salve in itself. I feel like I just won the celestial lottery. You've given me hope. I was this gun-carrying street kid from Brooklyn. When I think of you, I smile. I want to know you. I felt safe with you last night. You are my guidepost. Nobody else was there but you. I have to be real because I know, you'll take nothing else."

It was difficult to believe he was talking about me. His words so beautiful, I wrote them down, tears rolling down my face. "I never thought I could have an effect like this on someone…know that you touched me," I said.

"Maybe I'm not meant to marry…if we never talk again, know that you touched me."

We said our goodbyes and hung up. I wept, overwhelmed by all I had heard. He poured out every emotion he had. And…I gave it all right back.

I wiped my tears, and as I picked up the phone to call Ray, I couldn't help but think I had just made a mistake.

28

In the summer of 1999, after finishing my coursework at the G.T.U, I traveled to Kansas City, MO to do youth ministry. There, I sent a general email to my friends and received an email from Shawn. We hadn't spoken in months. He had just won the East Bay Poetry Slam Finals and would become one of the members of the Oakland Slam Team that would compete in Chicago that summer. Later in the email, he mentioned our kiss:

> …I am very happy that I got to experience that moment with you. It may never happen again, but that was very magical to me. I care about you a great deal, whether you know it or not. I hope that you are happy, and truth be told…you still have a place in my heart.

Shawn

Very formally, I responded:

Shawn,
This is very sweet of you. I know that you care about me. Know that I care about you, as well. I know that it probably was not easy for you to come to terms with this whole thing. I am quite grateful that somehow you are still able to keep a special place in you heart for me, in spite of the fact that I decided to date someone else. Ray and I broke up and are working on being friends.

Janet

╬

Shortly after returning to the Bay, Shawn and I had dinner and later walked to Lake Merritt where we sat on a park bench overlooking the lake. The moon and the city lights reflected off the lake's surface. A cool breeze brushed passed our faces. We could hear the faint sounds of ducks and geese in the distance. Shawn and I talked about how our summers went and later arrived at the topic of ministry and how we both viewed our work as ministry: he as a performer, and I as a youth minister and soon-to-be high school teacher. There was a brief silence before Shawn took my hand and held me as we danced in the glimmer of lake's reflection. And when we sat, he leaned toward me, gently kissing me above the temple.

As a little girl, I often daydreamt of a kiss like this. It seemed sweeter and more romantic than a kiss on the lips. I believed that the first man to kiss me in that perfect spot would be the man I would marry. And when Shawn kissed me, I instantly remembered this childhood fantasy.

╬

That night, on August 20, 1999, Shawn and I officially started dating. For our first few months together, whenever I looked at him, I couldn't help but be reminded of the Shepardsons. Two people, during a single summer, gave me the love that I didn't know I needed…which gave birth to my first poem reflecting my newly discovered self-love. And here I was, with the man I'd fallen in love with—a man that I might not have met if I hadn't read that poem at La Peña. One act of love has infinite effects.

And when I learned of Shawn's spirituality, I was reminded of Diego. Through our friendship, Diego helped me gain a great respect for and interest in the ways God manifests Godself through indigenous religious and cultural traditions. Because of our relationship, I was ready to fully accept Shawn, learning and respecting the ways in which his image of our ancestors and of God had been shaped by Hopi traditions, Kemetic science, and Afro-Caribbean religions. I had to acknowledge the overwhelming influence that Christianity had on the world and make sure my actions didn't reflect its institutional arrogance; this meant not having the desire to convert him to Catholicism. He was too beautiful to change.

‡

Throughout our relationship, we were struck by the impact we had on each other, never wanting to jeopardize the love we shared. Plagued with the possibility of losing him, I often cried, telling him, "I love you so much. But everyone I've ever loved died. I don't know what I would do if anything ever happened to you. I'm almost afraid to try loving again, in fear of eventually losing you."

Shawn had a similar fear. He believed our relationship was too good to be true. To him, it felt too right and therefore something was bound to interfere, causing our relationship to fall apart. Both of us were so accustomed to lives filled with tragedy that to have something good enter our lives was unforeseeable. Once we found a good thing, we were almost quick to reject it.

Afraid, yet confident I was *the one* for him, he proposed to me several times during our first year of dating. He once said, "My grandfather used to tell me, 'Boy, when you find a woman who makes your soul smile, you've found the right one.' And you make me smile. I have never been happier." Indeed, I was happy with him, as well, however, I wasn't as sure about marrying him as he was; so, I asked him to wait and propose to me once we'd dated a year.

He didn't care. He waited, knowing he wanted us to share our lives together, holding onto an image of what he wanted for us: a big house and a comfortable lifestyle free of worry over bills. On a couple occasions, I found him curled up in his bedroom. "I want to give you so much more than this," he said, weeping, "But I don't have much. I want to give you more. I'm sorry." But Shawn didn't see how much he'd already given me.

Besides his sense of humor, imagination, charisma, and lack of inhibitions, I was most fascinated with Shawn's integrity. He was the most honest person I'd ever met. He never spared anyone the truth, even if it meant sacrificing their feelings. In spite of finding him to be abrasive at times, I thought his approach to truth telling was definitely more effective in cases where gentle truth telling may only feel like a slap on the wrist, yielding no results. He was skilled at debates and clowning people without hesitation. He often defended women being harassed by men, not being afraid of a physical confrontation; at the same time, he could easily correct a person's racist remarks or rude behavior by flooring them with an insult from which the person couldn't recover; and sometimes you may see him snatching a cigarette from a person's mouth, yelling, "You nasty motherfucker!"

I admired his skill in confrontation partly because it was a gift I didn't naturally possess, and partly because I saw the immediate respect given to Shawn by the most arrogant, condescending assholes that made the mistake of challenging him. He said the things that people wished they could say, virtually turning strangers into instant friends.

Shawn was a firm believer that people should be held accountable for their bad behavior. Where most of us may "let things slide" to avoid a conflict, Shawn would immediately call out a person if they said or did something inconsiderate or hate-filled toward him or another individual. He did this because he believed in community— how our actions as human beings constantly affect each other. And for this reason, he believed it was absolutely necessary for us to be aware of the impact our action or inaction have on those we interacted with.

Shawn's longing for a greater, more just connection amongst people turned him into a natural healer. Besides holding others accountable, he also made sure his own actions were as selfless as possible. People often went to him for advice because he had a visionary's wisdom and because he would be completely honest.

Shawn had given me more than I could have ever imagined. He was the epitome of courage, passion, and purity of heart. His spirit meant more to me than any material possession he could give me.

On August 20, 2000, for our one-year anniversary, I took him to Bistro Viola, one of our favorite restaurants in Berkeley. That evening, we prepared to look our best: Shawn's face was smooth, with a striking, well-groomed goatee; he wore jet black pants with a mahogany long sleeve knit shirt that I bought for him—the one he didn't like because it made him feel like Bill Cosby. I wore a white chemise with a long black skirt and heels. As I put on my burgundy lipstick and fixed my hair, having two dark curls fall against my cheeks, I imagined how perfect the night of our engagement was going to be.

As we walked in, the restaurant was dim; champagne glasses and elegantly folded napkins were placed on every table; couples were smiling, leaning toward each other, the flicker of tealights reflecting off their faces. The host greeted us and led us out to the patio area which was partially lit by the sunset through the transparent canopy above. We sat down and looked at our menus. I could barely concentrate on what to order because I was guessing how Shawn was going to propose. Was he going to do it now? Was he going to kneel? Was he going to do it while we waited for our food? Maybe while we're eating dinner…or after dessert…

Our meals arrived: Shawn's grilled salmon and my garlic mussels. We ate and smiled and talked and laughed and ate. Still, he hadn't asked me. Then we shared dessert: crème bruleé. Again, we ate and smiled and talked and laughed and ate. Still no proposal.

I was so full. I could barely move. We paid for dinner and left the restaurant. It was 9:30 p.m. Still nothing. I grew impatient. Walking to the car, holding his hand, I asked, "Weren't you going to propose today?"

"Don't worry, I'll do it in my own time…You lost your chance!" he said laughing, getting me back for all the times I made him to wait for my answer.

⧉

A couple months later, I was in the kitchen, when Shawn knocked on the door, yelling, "Open the door! It's heavy! I need some help!" I was wondering what he was carrying. Were they boxes? Was it furniture?

When I opened the door, I only saw his arm. Hiding by the door, stretching out his hand, he held a red velvet box. He stepped in front of me and asked, "Will you marry me?"

Opening the box, I hugged and kissed him. "Yes," I said, slowly placing the ring on my finger.

29

After years of wanting to visit my mother's homeland in Labangon, I finally found the opportunity—and the money. I was ready to learn more about Momma and where she grew up. I wanted to find out about my grandparents and my aunts and uncles and cousins. I wanted to picture how they were as people—were they smart, were they fierce, were they *kuripot*, were they generous—all in hopes of getting clues to maybe explain the roots of my own personality traits.

Three days before my trip, I started packing. In the livingroom while I was kneeling on the floor folding my clothes, Shawn was lying on the couch, watching television. When I looked at him, he had a stark, blank look on his face.

"Shawn," I called to him, "Shawn. Shawn!" He finally snapped out of his trance. "What's wrong?" I asked.

"Your mom. I saw your mom's ghost. She came in from the sliding door, looked at me, and then disappeared into the wall."

Momma was with us. We were silent. This wasn't the first time she had appeared to him. Shawn had seen her many times; whereas I had never seen her once. I figured Momma came to let us know she would guide my travels or maybe came to bid me an early farewell before returning to her homeland.

The last time I visited the Philippines was when I was 5 years old. I had memories of *puto* wrapped in banana leaves and *tablea* heated in black iron kettles; of burning wood and humid air; of Momma putting make-up on my face and taking pictures of me dressed up in my cousin's yellow beauty pageant dress and her rhinestone tiara, which got stuck in my hair.

I was eager to see all of my relatives again, especially Auntie Adela, my mother's sister-in-law and dearest friend—the woman Momma wrote to religiously after she moved to the United States.

⌗

"Okay, Jinit," Auntie Adela said as we stepped out of the cab in front of her house. Auntie's house was made of wood and corrugated steel. On the bottom floor, the wall didn't quite reach the sides of the roof. She took me up the wooden stairs, to a room she had prepared just for me. "This is your room Jinit. You will estay here. We rented an air conditioner for you, ha. I know, you are American, so you need aircon."

"Wow, thank you, Auntie," I said, amazed, "You didn't have to rent an air conditioner," knowing she didn't have that much money. I didn't even have an air conditioner in my own apartment back home, I thought. Looking around the room, I noticed the bed was nicely made with Strawberry Shortcake bedsheets and a pillowcase to match. In the corner stood a wooden shelf with photos of me that Momma sent to her over fifteen years ago. Next to the air conditioner was a dresser with rubbing alcohol, cotton swabs, and other toiletries on top. Moved at the thought of how much care she took in preparing this room for me, all I could say was thank you.

Even though I was exhausted from the fourteen-hour plane ride, I was eager to see the rest of Labangon. Auntie Adela was eager, too. So, as soon as I put away my suitcase and changed clothes, we took a walk down Salvador Street.

The road was paved but had no lanes and no traffic signals. *Tricycads* and motorcycles and *jeepneys* whizzed by. *Sari-sari* stores were open all along the street—people were selling sour mangos with *hipon*, fried plantains, fresh bowls of *sinigang* and *dugo dugo*. *Manangs* crouched low, sharpening skewers one-by-one only to sell them for a few pesos a bundle. The smell of diesel gas, ashes from burnt trash, and smoke from *lechon* sat thick on the air. And as we kept walking, I noticed my people's complexions ranging from fair to dark brown. I stared at the dark and beautiful faces—faces that still bore resemblance to the Aeta, the indigenous inhabitants of the Philippines.

As we walked, Auntie kept asking me, "Are you thirsty? Are you hungry? Maybe, let's buy something to drink. What do you want?"

"No, I'm fine, Auntie," I said politely.

A few minutes later, she asked again, "Jinit, do you want something to drink? You are not thirsty? You are not hungry?"

I finally gave in and decided to buy something. "Uh, okay, I'll get something." I approached one of the *sari-sari* stores and asked the man if he had juice. The man handed me a juice pack that looked like a Capri Sun. By the time I reached in my pocket for some money, Auntie Adela had already paid for it. That's how it was during the entire trip with every meal, every snack, and every cab and *jeepney* ride—I never paid a dime while I was there. It wasn't that Auntie Adela was wealthy. Actually, she was amongst the poorest in the *barangay*. But, it was just natural for her to be this hospitable, this welcoming.

Auntie Adela was a very vibrant, elegant, forthright woman in her sixties who never took "No" for an answer. She was tall, with no gray hair and a supple face, free of wrinkles. She had a little restaurant called "Auntie Adela's

Canteen" where she served food right outside her front door to all the students from the high school across the street. Whenever leaving the house, she wore sharp dress suits, looking as though she worked for the government or for a big company. She paid for everything with money she didn't have and slipped a few pesos to anyone willing to grant a favor. She was a hustler who knew how to get things done...with class...quickly and quietly.

As she introduced me to everyone on the streets of Labangon, I became slightly embarrassed. "This is Inday Lucy's daughter!"

"Oh she's so big now," old friends of my mother said, "You look just like your mom!" Other passers-by needed no introduction, as they whispered, "*Ikaw tong anak ni Inday Lucy?*" as if my face was proof enough.

Yes, Momma left her imprint on me in more ways than one. Once, Auntie and I were eating lunch at the Metro, a mall in Cebu City. Afterward, I was so full but still had some *puso* left over. I wrapped it in a napkin and slipped it into my purse.

"My God," Auntie said, smiling, "I'm looking at Inday Lucy!" We laughed. I had no idea my mom wrapped her leftovers, too. Actually, I couldn't even recall watching her do that as a child. I felt a little twinge at the thought of inheriting my mother's habits without even being in her presence. I guess my mother never did leave me.

⚓

"Here's some rice, here, o," Auntie said, as she put some on my plate, "You eat. There's some *lumpia*, some *dugo dugo*, some vegetables..." I filled my plate with every dish on the table and started eating with my hands.

"O, you know how to eat with your hands?" Auntie said.

"Yeah. Do you mind if I eat with my hands?" I asked.

"No, that's how we eat before because we don't have any spoon and fork."

"When I was little, I tried eating with my hands like my mom. But I was too messy…so my mom wouldn't let me. I didn't really start eating with my hands until I moved in with Auntie Pacita and Tatay…because everybody in the house ate with their hands."

As we sat together, I learned quickly that Auntie Adela was the keeper of all stories—the stories lost in secrets, the stories no one wanted to remember, the stories her neighbors already knew. These stories were her life's blood.

"Your *lolo*," Auntie said, holding a handful of rice, "He liked very much the carpentry. Like a screwdriver. He has a small one up to the bigger one. And the saw. Small one and the bigger one. He did not like always to let someone borrow dat, borrow dat, because he might need to use dat. You can use dat, *but* you have to return dat in its place…the proper place, where you get dat. And once you get dat and return it to *another* place, it is a very big story! Yeah! That is your *lolo's* character. That's mine, also…I got that from your *lolo*. Your mom, too."

"It's funny because that's how my mom was with me. I could never touch anything unless I made sure I put it back where I found it. You know, I also remember, my mother never let me put plates at the edge of the table…just in case they might get knocked over. And if I did, I got in big trouble."

"…O, and there's also one time when she got mad at your Uncle Tinong…Uncle Tinong left his daughter,

Marie, at her house. And everytime there was a…personal appearance of a celebrity, a star, she never missed it. She always brought me. So, your mom told me we go to downtown. We did not bring Marie. We left Marie with your *lola*. And Marie, she had, what is dat…a deep bite. When we came back home, Tinong was so angry, 'You did not care about Marie's feet. There were so many flies eating that bite…' So your mom got mad also, 'You're the father, you're the one to care for your child…you are not doing anything all day…' She got mad. Why she was blamed? Why didn't he put a bandage on dat so it cannot be eaten by the flies? Tinong always blamed your mom. So, your Uncle Tinong was getting angry. Your mom also getting angry. Then, your mom get inside…in the kitchen. 'Oh,' your mom shouted, 'Oh, get inside here,' she got a *bolo*, 'get inside here, so I can hack you!!"

I laughed so hard. "Ha, I can just see my mom holding the *bolo*…" I said, immediately reminded of how she chased away that baseball player with a stick.

"And at this time," Auntie continued, "your mom was writing to your dad. But your mom did not tell us. The time that she told us was the time when he arrived. And that was the time when we were out. She was afraid of your *lolo*. She did not think that your *lolo* could accept your dad. She didn't say she had a penpal; she did not even tell her mother. Because she did not experience ever having a boyfriend."

"No, boyfriend, at all?" I asked.

"No, boyfriend."

"But there were a lot of people who courted her right?" I persisted.

"No, not even that. They were ashamed."

"Because she was from a well-to-do family?"

"Oo, yeah…maybe some guys wanted to court your mom…but she was from a well-to-do family and your mom was not an easy girl like others. She was very educated…That's why when we know she had a penpal, most of the people here were very surprised.

"So when I and your mom came home, a neighbor came running, 'Oh! Inday Lucy. There's a foreigner at your house. He came to see you!' She was so nervous and walked so fast.   Your *lolo* and your dad were sitting outside talking and enjoying. Your *lolo* was impressed by your dad since he flew all the way from the United States to meet your mom.

"Then Lita, your mom's sister, was yelling at your dad across the street, 'A buffalo! An American buffalo!' Your dad said, 'What did she say?' But you *lolo* did not answer…and then your mom tried to avoid your *lolo* and your dad and she run past the house to go hide. Your dad said, 'Oh, Lucy!' and she stopped and turned around.

"And when they got married, they came back to your *lolo* and *lola's* house. Maria, her friend from City Hall, was the one to come forward to tell them Inday Lucy got married. Your mom and dad stood behind.   Your *lolo* and *lola* accepted it…"

And according to Auntie Adela, when Momma left for the United States, my grandparents were very happy for her. However, unfortunately, not everyone was as happy as they were.

As Auntie Adela told me about Lita's reaction to Momma's marriage, she got up from the table, opened up a box of files and pulled out a letter written by Lita in 1970.

She translated this letter for me one word at a time. "Here ay, this is the letter I told you about. This is what your Auntie Lita wrote to your *lolo*. It says here ay, 'Congratulations, your daughter has married an American.

But what kind of an American is he. He is a Black…a Black American is at the bottom of all the Americans…'"

As she continued reading it, the contempt she had for this woman was clear; her face was tense as she grew louder, having a slight quiver in her voice. Auntie Adela was angry and had stayed angry for over thirty years. She stayed angry because she didn't want anyone to forget the pain Lita caused the whole family. It was as though she felt it her duty to remain angry—for my mother's sake.

We later walked upstairs to my room to enjoy the cool breeze from the air conditioner. Our heads met as we laid on the bed together, reminiscing about my mother. "You know this reminds me of how I and your mom used to always lie down on the bed together and talk," Auntie said, smiling with a brightness in her eye, "When I was young and the kids were small, I could not go out during the day. So your mom, apter work, would always bisit me and tell me the latest news." I laid there listening, thinking how strange it was that decades later, I was lying down next to her now, sharing secrets and stories as she and my mom once did. And I thought of every story Auntie told me and how all the questions that I was too young to ask when Momma and Da'y were alive were answered. Auntie Adela gave me the history I was missing. And these stories were passed down to me by a woman who missed my mom just as much as I did.

YOU AND I

I dreamt of the U.S.
What it would be like?

On the plane,
Over land and water
I was
High on dreams
On tantalizing tales
Luring me with gazes,
And visions of mazes
Through the
Land of milk and honey
Where I would give birth to you
These are my dreams:
We would go to the park and have picnics
And be greeted by white faces
In my new home
Home is the United States.
Where I would be happy.
I would be happy.

And, *anak* I was so happy with you.
You and I
We picked cans together
Pulled on our latex gloves
And dug in every trash can in the park

Plunged our hands
Through shitty diapers and ripped-up pornography
Half-eaten hot dogs and hamburger buns
All for five aluminum cans

Five aluminum cans
We smashed to the rhythm
Of my fluctuating heartbeat that weakened
Every time I watched your little hand reach in the trash

And quickened
Every time we found a can

And weakened
When I asked that white guy, "Are you throwin' that
away?"
And quickened
When I chased him with my stick
After he told me to go back where I came from.

You thought we were just picking cans
When we were picking soft rubies
And crushing them beneath our feet
Crushing our hearts, squeezing out the dignity
And selling them for 40 cents a pound
I was fighting a private revolution
Revolving around me, the trash can and my new
homeland

But *anak*, I was so happy with you.
You and I,
We watched Johnny Carson together
Until you fell asleep and
I scribbled Johnny's jokes on the bottom of tissue boxes
So in the morning I could tell you what he said.
We shared jokes for breakfast

So my evening dose of solace
Could extend into the next day

Am I trying to escape or be in the moment?

I don't know,
But in the moment,
You and I
We forget the conventional use of this tissue box

You thought I was just watching Johnny,

When I was resting from battle,
I was tired of yells and fights,
Of empty bank accounts,
Social insecurity checks,
Medi-Cal share of costs,
Sibling hate rupturing my internal respite

The reverie interrupted...

Now a thousand of my cries lay upon one empty breath
Trying to come to revelations upon revolutions
Spun in circles searching for resolutions

I, now, aware
That I belonged anywhere
His jokes would take me.
As long as I was happy,
I was happy.

But *anak*, I was so happy with you.
You and I
We are apart, now.
And we're here together.
But, you can't see me in this cramped grave.

I'm pulling my homeland from the trash can
To see if Johnny will make me laugh now.
I plunge my hands through
Shacks and broken glass,
Squatter fear and *tsismosas*,
All for five remaining memories of my homeland.

Hoping you can redeem them
For more than 40 cents a pound
More than happiness

Redeem them for my blood.
Redeem them for our hearts

The ones we crushed in the park together.

Anak, I was so happy with you.

30

 With a little over an hour to get ready, I quickly swallowed some left over sandwiches from the bridal shower and walked upstairs to soak my feet. Warm water filled the tub as I poured in some foot soap. I planned to be barefoot for our wedding, so it was important that my feet didn't look like claws. Sitting on the side of the tub, I placed my feet in the water, and exhaled. Massaging each toe and the arches of my feet, I rubbed on some Corn Husker's Lotion, smelling the scent that reminded me of how Mom and Da'y once used this lotion to soften their own feet. With a pumice stone, I scrubbed my feet until they were soft. Then I took a long, warm shower, lathering down, shaving my legs, washing my hair.

 After placing my engagement ring on my middle toe, I painted my toenails and waited for them to dry. Before putting on my dress, the phone rang:

 "Hello," I said.

 "Hi, honey," Tom said, "We just wanted to let you know we're on our way."

 "Okay. You know how to get here right…" I asked, later verifying the directions.

 "Yes, okay, we'll see you in a few minutes. Love you, honey."

 I finally pulled on my wedding gown: it was sleeveless with satin lining beneath a layer of lace; pearls and sequins glimmered from every angle; like an evening gown, the dress hugged my body, having a long slit in the back; what was originally a train, I clipped to a comb and turned into a veil which would drape around my face and wrap around my shoulders like a shawl.

When searching for my wedding dress the previous year, I knew I wasn't just choosing a dress for myself. The gown had to be unique enough, elegant enough, to be handed down to my children. Since I didn't have the benefit of wearing my grandmother's wedding dress or my mother's wedding dress (like some women speak of), I decided to be that mother or that grandmother who would pass on her wedding dress to her descendants. And yes, this gown was lovely enough to be passed down to my future children.

When the Shepardsons arrived, I threw on a white robe and ran outside to open the gate. Immediately inviting them in, I opened my robe to let them take a peek. The kids became excited and quickly hugged me. On the verge of tears, Diana's face brightened. Tom looked at me with a mild expression as if watching his first-born get married. Diana was helping me button up my dress when her tears finally fell. I cried, too, feeling Katie's arms wrapped around me. It was a sacred time for us—a pivotal moment marking the transition from the single life to the married life—a moment usually shared between a mother and her daughter.

I carefully put on the veil and wrapped it around my shoulders. The Shepardsons took a final look at me before we left for the ceremony. Tom held me gently by the shoulders and said, "Honey, we are so proud of you..." My new dad was proud of me...was happy for me. As he looked at me, I felt like that little girl who used to sit in the second row of his World History class, quickly taking notes, eagerly raising my hand to answer questions. And at the same time, I wasn't that little girl. He could see that I had grown into a young woman, gazing upon me as if Da'y was staring through his eyes.

As we piled into the van, I got into the front seat. I took a deep breath and felt Tom's hand take mine, telling me how special and sacred this moment was for him, as well as for his family.

╬

Tall redwoods towered overhead, leaving an open clearing below. The sun attempted to spill through the trees but was caught by the branches, allowing only scattered rays to hit the ground. Separated by no more than a single step, one could either feel the comfort of the trees' shelter or the warmth of the afternoon sun. Birds sang songs and glided from tree to tree seeming to enjoy their home as much as their guests did. The grass and clovers of emerald green lay beneath the various species of plants and bushes that surrounded us as though we were standing in Rivendell in *Lord of the Rings*.

Shawn and his best men, Naru and Robert, arranged the brown folding chairs in a large circle and planted bamboo torches around the reception area to ward off any unwelcome insects. Robert cleared the sharp twigs and rocks from the long, dirt pathway, the aisle that the bridesmaids and I would soon walk down. Lisa and Gina, two of my bridesmaids, covered the picnic tables with navy blue tablecloth and white satin napkins at the center; adding the final touches to the centerpieces, they took the round glass bowls that were filled with smooth rocks and pine cones and poured water into each one; blackberries, raspberries, and white rose petals were dropped in to float and mingle with the pine cones while a gardenia-shaped candle was gently placed on top.

As the guests arrived—Mama Lila, Ms. Weidemann, Lou, Brenda, and several others—the flickering centerpieces, the scent of pine, and the gentle sounds of a guitar welcomed them, and one could see an immediate calm come over their faces when entering the sacred space.

"Now, you'll be standing here," Emilio, our priest and friend, explained, "facing Shawn, like this."

"Am I on the right side…" I began to ask when Lee, Gina's husband, approached us, holding the video camera.

"Excuse me…Janet…can I see your feet?"

I stuck out the foot with the engagement ring on it. Lee zoomed in on my bare foot. "There we go. There we go," he laughed.

Once Emilio finished giving me the last minute details before the ceremony, he left to tend to Shawn. I stood alone in the shade, holding my bouquet of white lilies. Feeling the dirt and pebbles between my toes and marveling at the trees, I prayed and waited until Emilio gave me the sign. I was pleased to watch Lou and Tom as they walked toward me. If Da'y could not walk me down the aisle, then having them, the two men who had always cared for me, was the next best thing. The three of us stood in the shade quietly. Every now and then I'd say a little something to Lou and then leaned to my left to speak to Tom; they said little to each other. Tom held my hand, gently stroking it, and I leaned against Lou, our shoulders touching. A comforting silence filled those final few moments before the ceremony.

Shawn, Naru, and Robert walked around the circle of guests—forty of our closest friends and relatives—cleansing the space with burning sage. Emilio gave the signal and the wedding march began.

With Tom on my left and Lou on my right, we marched down the aisle to meet Shawn. As we drew closer, we saw the guests standing. At the shrine made in memory of my parents and Shawn's uncle and grandfather, the candle flickered, telling us that they, too, were bearing witness to the ceremony. The groomsmen were huddled around Shawn; and then they turned around. Shawn, in his silk navy blue *guayabera*, was in tears. When I saw him, my eyes also welled up. Lou and Tom unlaced their arms from mine and embraced Shawn before taking their seats. Slowly, Shawn and I took each other's hands, looking deeply into one another's eyes.

"In the name of Janet and Shawn," Emilio began, "I welcome you all to this joyous celebration of their sacred union. Their prayer today, in the presence of their family and friends, is that our loving Creator may seal and strengthen their love. It was very important for them that you be here…that they do this publicly in the presence of not only you, the people who have loved them into being, but also that of their ancestors from several continents and religious beliefs. These are the women and men, through which God has blessed them and now graces them with this special sacrament so that they may live the rest of their lives in this sacred union.

"Janet and Shawn have chosen to have their wedding here, in nature, in creation, because it is the place where God often revealed Godself to them, either in times of family picnics or quiet moments of contemplation and vision quests. In a special way this holy day, they want you to feel Mother Earth, Father Sky, Sister Moon, and Brother Sun…the cleansing with sage marks this as a safe place for us to be…as a sacred site, asking humble permission to use it, so that we experience the sacredness which is God in all things and all things in God. Water, touch, the rings…all of these are sacred symbols in our tradition.

"And now they will pour libations into Mother Earth, honoring their ancestors as when we light a candle or incense before a picture of one of our loved ones who has gone home to God."

"We would like to pour libations," Shawn began, "for our ancestors and those who have recently passed: Roy McConnell, Levinia McConnell, and Maurice McConnell," pouring water into the earth.

"…and Lucrecia Mendoza Stickmon, Fermon Stickmon, and Pacita Tabasa," I added, pouring the water. "We would like to call upon all those living who could not be with us today and ask that their spirits be present with us in our hearts," I said, pouring the water a final time.

"Let us pray in gentle silence as we enter into the giftedness of life," Emilio proclaimed, "Gracious and loving God, when you created humankind, you willed that man and wife should be one. Bind Janet and Shawn in the loving union of marriage and make their love fruitful so that they may be living witnesses to your divine love in the world. We ask this Jesus, brother of all and prince of peace."

Shawn and I sat arm-in-arm as we listened to the reading from 1 Corinthians 13: 1-8. I took in the passage and when I heard the verses, "It [Love] bears all things, believes all things, hopes all things, endures all things. Love never fails," I felt confident that our love would grow strong, in spite of those who doubted our relationship would last due to our different religious backgrounds.

Then, Golda, Shawn's good friend and my third bridesmaid, began to sing:

Swimming circles
Like the waves…upon the shore of me…
Incessantly, you call to me, to break the fever, burning me…

Her voice was dreamlike, weaving in and out of the circle, blurring the space between traditional church hymns and the songs of Björk and Esthero, creating a spiritual vibe reminding me of that first time I saw Shawn perform at *Soul Searches*.

As her song came to an end, Emilio stood to begin his homily. "…I guess it was about two weeks ago we got together in Berkeley, and we talked about how we wanted to do this. And Janet and Shawn shared with me, why this place was so special…why they wanted to have it outside and why the symbols we're using today. And as I mentioned I had taught Janet. As she was talking…there was a lot of feeling there…I could picture her sitting in my office…I could picture her when we were having a beer at local bar…I could picture all these memories, and I thought of the first time I met Shawn. And then I thought about what I would say about Shawn because I didn't want this little sermon to be lopsided…so…inside myself I said, help me Lord, help me to know the passion that is behind this man and this woman who now are doing this special event in the presence of God, in your presence here with Mother Nature. So one of the things I asked them was, 'What readings have you chosen? What do you want to read?' They told me about this letter of Paul that was just read. I thought to myself, of all the things in our Judeo-Christian tradition, why this? And they said, 'It is very real.' I said yes, yes, but give me more…professors are always wanting more…and then I heard about the people who inspired them to take this important step, some of the ancestors we heard mentioned. I heard about Shawn's grandparents who spent 56 years together; recollections of a 6'7" 'lunatic' grandfather; Janet's parents whose love embraced the riches of Filipino and African-American cultures. Like Paul, they had been loved into being…especially when they couldn't see this love and beauty in themselves.

"So, why this confidence? How is it that two people can have this confidence…that two people can commit themselves for better or for worse...in sickness and in health? Well, they've tasted it. Through sacred rituals, they know creation as life-giving and holy. They come from holy traditions which value community and simplicity, commitment to justice, and dignity for every human person. And I'm sure they have their fears, but which one of us doesn't…but because of what they have seen and heard, they are able to love each other....And now I would like to invite Shawn and Janet to stand. In the presence of God and this community, Shawn and Janet have some very important things to say to each other…"

Shawn and I stood with the wedding party beside us. Facing one another, holding hands, we exchanged vows. "I, Shawn Taylor, take you, Janet Mendoza Stickmon, to be my wife. My support and love are yours, always. I will be open with you, honest with you, and will do all that I can to ensure our happiness now and in the future. I am so happy to be marrying my best friend—to have and to hold, for better or worse, in sickness and in health, for the rest of our lives."

"I, Janet Mendoza Stickmon, take you, Shawn Taylor, to be my husband. I promise to always love and give you my support. I promise to always be honest and open with you, bringing us closer to each other, letting nothing come between us. I want to grow with you and grow old together. I know there is a piece of you in me that needs only you to bring out that beauty. You make me feel beautiful. And I am so happy to be marrying my best friend to have and to hold, for better or worse, for richer, for poorer, in sickness and in health, for the rest of our lives."

Shawn and I were both crying. Emilio hands me a handkerchief. I wiped my tears and then wiped Shawn's. His nose was running and I whispered to him, "Here, do you want to wipe it?"

"No, you can wipe it," he whispered back. I tried wiping his nose without laughing, but couldn't resist. Handing the handkerchief to Shawn, he blew his nose. Emilio laid his hand on Shawn's shoulder, asking him, "Are you gonna make it?"

"Yeah," he said, shaking it off and bouncing like a boxer. Shawn attempted to hand the handkerchief back to Emilio.

"No," Emilio said, smiling, "Consider it a gift." All of us laughed.

While blessing the rings with sprinkles of water, Emilio said, "God, we ask that you bless these rings…may Janet and Shawn always do your will and always live together in peace, goodwill, and love."

Emilio handed Shawn's ring to me, and I said, "Shawn, take this ring as a sign of my love and fidelity."

Then Shawn took my hand and said, "Janet, take this ring as a sign of my love and fidelity."

"And may the love that Janet and Shawn share be spread to all those who love them," Emilio concluded, inviting our guests to applaud. Shawn and I kissed and moved toward the center of the circle, as my friend from F.S.T., Rawn, began to sing:

> *I promise love for you always.*
> *Believing in you, there's no end.*
> *You are my sweetheart forever.*
> *You are God's gift, my best friend.*
> *You are the light I am guided by,*
> *Giving me a place to be free.*
> *With your love, I can touch the sky,*

Against all odds, you and me.

My life, I give.
My whole soul, I give.
We will remain as one for life.
Honoring you as my love.

My life, I give…

We held each other as we listened to our song; Shawn and I wrote these lyrics, asking Rawn to sing them to the tune of his song, "Come to the Table of Mercy." And as it came to an end, Rawn looked at Shawn and I, bowing his head before us.

Emilio invited our guests to rise and lay their hands upon us to offer their blessings and wisdom. The hands of forty of the most beautiful people in our lives reached toward the center, touching our bodies, infusing us with a loving power. Their grace-filled energy radiated from the circle, willing for us, through their words and touch, a long life of love and honesty and selflessness. From people who had known us as children to the friends we had met as adults, we were all interconnected in that moment. How profound it was to know that the people we shared a history with chose to witness our wedding. Perhaps, it was even more profound to know that the beautiful people we had grown so fond of had the chance to finally meet each other.

31

The bell rang for lunch. I grabbed my sandwich and chips out of my backpack and sat down at one of the desks. Cheryl, one of my former students, walked in with her usual smile, "Hi, Ms. Stickmon! How are you?"

"Oh, I'm fine. How you doin'?"

"I'm fine. Just thought I'd stop by for awhile and talk."

I knew this meant she had a lot on her mind and wanted to pick up where we left off the last time we spoke. Meanwhile, Brandon, Jeff, and Mandingo all walked in the room, "Hey, wassup, Ms. Stickmon," they said in unison, as they immediately made their way toward my CD player. A few other guys walked in and within minutes, they started a cypher.

Cheryl and I decided to move to another corner of the room. As we were talking, out of the corner of my eye, I could see Fernando, a student from my religion class, waiting for me near the door. He was always too polite to interrupt so I said, "Cheryl, can you excuse me for a second?"

"Sure, no problem," she said.

Looking at Fernando, I asked, "Hey! How are you? Did you want to ask me something?"

"Yeah. Can you help me with a geometry problem? I've been tryin' to figure this thing out, and I can't quite get it."

"Sure," I said, as he pulled up a seat next to us. I began to help him and found that I was stuck. Cheryl knew the key equation that I had forgotten. With that, all three of us ended up figuring out the problem together. For a split second, I scanned the room and noticed how much was going on. Circled up near my desk, the guys still had the cypher going, rhymin' and noddin' their heads to the beats of the East Flatbush Project on my raggedy gray stereo. Anthony was B-boyin' at the center of the room, trying to show some of his moves to his friend, Kenny. And I was sitting there having a conversation with one student, helping another with a math problem, and bobbin' my head to the beat all at the same time. This is a snapshot of my typical day teaching at a high school in Richmond, CA.

After graduating from the G.T.U, my desire to counsel priests and nuns was placed on hold when I found a job as a high school teacher. It's been six years now, and I have learned so much in the time I've spent teaching algebra, social justice, history of Christianity, and spoken word. There's no other place I'm more comfortable than with high school students. And if my students collected all the images they have of Ms. Stickmon during class, lunchtime, a club meeting, and after school, they'd have the clearest picture of me. With about 150 students each day, I can be crazy, playful, candid, direct, serious, and gentle. At any given moment, my conversations with students can range from topics about racism, homophobia, and sexism to math, religion, and poetry. It's the only place where my versatility can be fully used and where my limitations can be sources of growth. At the same time, I can still have fun.

As for those moments when I can speak to my students one-on-one, I am always humbled and flattered by the personal details they trust me with. Every now and then, especially when I look at a student without parents, I see myself. And then time freezes...

Despite those who have tried using me as a poster child for what it means to "overcome life's obstacles," I have never expected adults or young people to "just get over" their problems. It would be foolish to trivialize the amount of courage, will, self-reflection, and change such an expectation requires. Attempting to live a healthy, love-filled life is no easy task, especially given some of the injustices that exist within our institutions and within our own families; it not only requires a person's relentless desire to live, but also the loving support of friends and relatives.

As I reflect upon my life, I see myself continuously chasing home: that which is familiar, comforting, and deeply connected to other human beings; that feeling that I am loved and that place where one mistake will not jeopardize my acceptance. I chase this place as if I know what it looks like, what it feels like, what it tastes like. And maybe I do. Perhaps I gauge what is home with respect to how similar an experience is to what I once felt in Momma and Da'y's presence. However, what's interesting is that all the places I've felt at home—with Mama Lila, Lou, the Shepardsons, friends from college, Anabelle and Gilberto, Auntie Adela, my students, with my husband, Shawn, and at times, within myself—have been vastly different from my childhood home.

I constantly toy with the idea that we, as human beings, have an internal desire to search for home, to be at home; that we have an intuitive sense within that tells us when we have found it...even when we have gone countless years without a home; that this sense of what is home grows and matures as we grow and mature.

In my constant desire to feel at home, I learned that I'd been looking too hard for a single home. Instead, I was blessed with several, as if to show that our spirits require far more space than one home can offer.

GLOSSARY

adobo: chicken or pork dish cooked in vinegar and soy sauce; recipe varies

anak: child (Tagalog)

aray: colloquial expression in Cebuano meaning ouch

bata: baby; *tata* or *ta* is sometimes given as a nickname (Visaya)

barangay: also called barrios; small communities or villages spread throughout the Philippine Islands

bolo: type of machete (Tagalog and Visaya)

Ikaw tong anak ni Inday Lucy?: Are you Inday Lucy's child? (Cebuano)

John Brown: a white abolitionist who led a slave revolt in Harpers Ferry, Virginia in 1859

bungol: deaf (Visaya)

Cebuano: Visayan language spoken in Cebu

dugo dugo: also known as dinuguan or chocolate meat; a Filipino dish made of pork and pork blood

hipon: salted shrimp paste

inday: a general term used to refer to a young girl (Visaya)

jeepney: mode of public transportation; the first jeepneys were made from scrapped World War II army jeeps

kababayan: fellow countryperson (Filipino)

kuripot: greedy, stingy (Tagalog)

lechon: roasted pig (Filipino and Visaya)

lola: grandmother (Filipino and Visaya)

lolo: grandfather (Filipino and Visaya)

lumpia: Filipino eggrolls usually filled with pork, onions, and garlic; filling varies *manang* (or *nang*): term used to address an elder sister (Visaya) or an older woman (Pilipino and Visaya)

oo: yes

pancit: commonly refers to pancit canton which is a dish made with flour sticks (i.e. flour noodles); *pancit bihon* or *bihon* refers to a dish made with rice sticks (i.e. thin rice noodles)

pho: Vietnamese rice noodle soup

puso: rice wrapped in coconut leaves (Visaya)

puto: a dessert made from sweet rice (Visaya)

the religious: a term often used by Catholics to refer to members of a Roman Catholic religious order

sanduk: to scoop rice out of the pot (or rice cooker) and onto someone's plate (Visaya)

sari-sari: translated as "various" or "variety" in Filipino (or Tagalog????) and Visaya; sari-sari stores refer to the stores often found in front of residents' homes where a variety of items ranging from food to bamboo sticks are sold (Tagalog and Visaya)

Singkil: a dance tracing its origin to the Maranao people of Mindanao which depicts the epic of the Darangan in which Princess Gandingan is caught in a forest during an earthquake that is caused by diwatas (deities); the princess moves gracefully through two pairs of clapped, criss-crossed bamboo poles representing trees falling as a result of the earthquake; she is accompanied by a waiting lady and later is rescued by a prince.

sinigang: fish or pork cooked in a tamarind soup base

tablea: large chocolate tablets heated in water to make a hot cocoa drink (Filipino)

tatay: daddy or father (Tagalog and Visaya)

Tinikling: the national dance of the Philippines which originated in Leyte; the dancers step and turn between two beaten bamboo poles, imitating the movement of the tiklíng (a bird native to rice paddies of the Philippines)

tricycad: a man-powered tricycle that transports passengers (Tagalog and Visaya)

tsismosa: a woman who gossips (Visaya)

Vinta: a Muslim dance that pays tribute to the Filipino ancestors who sailed in vintas (quick and agile boats with colorful sails) to Mindanao and the Sulu archipelago during the 12th century; while dancers with fans and scarves depict the waves of the ocean, a prince and princess balance on bamboo poles, imitating the movements of the vinta

Visaya: language family spoken in the Visayan Islands

whoopin' boy: a whooping boy was believed in Jamaica to be a duppie (or a spirit) found within the roots of cotton trees

Waray: Visayan language spoken in Samar, Leyte, & Biliran; also known as *Waray-Waray*

WORKS CITED

Garcia, Ben. *Visayan-English Vocabulary*. Cebu City: Ben Garcia, 1990.

Hesse, Hermann. *Siddhartha*. 1951. New York: Bantam Books, 1971.

Manalili, F. Macapinlac, et al. *English-Pilipino-Visaya Vocabulary*. Quezon City: R. Manalili GEN. MDSE., 1970.

Re: Collections. By The Pilipino American Alliance of University of California, Berkeley. Zellerbach Hall, University of California, Berkeley. 25 April, 1999.

Sagalongos, Felicidad T.E. *Diksiyunaryong Ingles-Pilipino, Pilipino-Ingles*. Mandayluyong City: National Bookstore, Inc., 1968.

Sargento, Golda. "Circles (Love)." Roberts Regional Park, Oakland. July 2002.

Sheed, F.J. *Theology for Beginners*. 3rd ed. Ann Arbor: Servant Books, 1981.

Solis, Melchizedek Maraon. *Pilipinas A to Z*. 1995. Salinas: SRMNK Publishers, 1999.

Tortello, Rebecca. "The Fall of a Gentle Giant-The Collapse of Tom Cringle's Cotton Tree." *Jamaica Gleaner* 25 Feb. 2002. 15 Oct. 2004 www.jamaica-gleaner.com/pages/history/story0020.html.

Tuttle, Kate. "John Brown." *Africana-The Encyclopedia of the African and African American Experience*. Ed. Kwame

Anthony Appiah and Henry Louis Gates, Jr. New York: Civitas Books, 1999.

Villame, Yoyoy. "My Country, The Philippines." 1988.

Wiley, Mark. *Filipino Martial Arts*. Vermont: Charles E. Tuttle Publishing Company, 1994.

ABOUT THE AUTHOR

Prof. Janet C. Mendoza Stickmon, author of *Crushing Soft Rubies* and *Midnight Peaches, Two O'clock Patience*, is a teacher, writer, and performer. Stickmon has taught ethnic studies, social justice, history of Christianity, spoken word and algebra at Salesian High School in Richmond, CA for several years. She is currently a professor of Humanities at Napa Valley College, teaching Filipina(o)-American Heritage, American Mind I and II, and Intro to Africana Studies. Prof. Stickmon is the founder and facilitator of Broken Shackle Developmental Training—a program that promotes the use of healing techniques to help reduce the effects of internalized racism. Stickmon's books have been used in courses at several colleges and universities across the country. She is also a spoken word artist who has performed at several venues across the country. Through her literature and performances, she explores issues of love, motherhood, resilience, ancestral connection, and joy. Stickmon holds a Master's of the Arts Degree in Ethnic Studies from San Francisco State University, a Master's of the Arts Degree in Religion and Society from the Graduate Theological Union in Berkeley, and a Bachelor's of Science Degree in Civil Engineering from the University of California, Irvine. Her work has influenced thousands of adults and adolescents for the last seventeen years.

For workshops, presentations, and products, visit
www.brokenshackle.wordpress.com or email
brokenshacklepublishing@gmail.com.

Made in the USA
Monee, IL
17 August 2022

11835161R00164